A Century of I
Staffordshire Buses

John Cooke

The Horizon Press

Published by
The Horizon Press
The Oaks, Moor Farm Road West, Ashbourne, DE6 1HD
Tel: (01335) 347349 Fax: (01335) 347303

1st Edition
13 ISBN: 978-1-84306-469-5

Print: CPI, Anthony Rowe, Chippenham
Design by: Michelle Prost

FRONT COVER: PMT Leyland PD3/4 Titan, H704 loads up by The Essoldo, Hanley.

REAR COVER (Top large): Tram replacement SOS 'QL' No.110, VT 809 was received on the 23rd March 1928 at Stoke. Five days later it was used by PET to demonstrate the innovative destination blind system to the Ministry of Transport and the 'Commercial Motor' trade magazine. This is one of a series showing an inspector and driver fitting the linen blind to the destination box of the Brush B37F body. No. 110 was withdrawn from service on 31st December 1936 and was sold to Beech, the Hanley dealer for £12/10/-. (PET/PMT)

REAR COVER (small): New PMT Bristol RESL6L/ECW B44F No.185, JEH 185K is guided round the Springfields Keelings Road roundabout by the author on a photo shoot for the PMT House Magazine in August 1971. This was the sixth Bristol, which arrived after Nationalisation had allowed PMT to have the type, to enter the fleet. This batch was the last to be delivered in PMT red and cream livery. It was withdrawn in December 1980 to Ensign, the dealers, who sold it on to Wooliscroft (Silver Service) of Darley Dale via North (dealer). (Alf Fallows/PMT)

A Century of North Staffordshire Buses

John Cooke

The Horizon Press

CONTENTS

BODY CODES

Before seating capacity:

H – High bridge double deck or low height with centre gangway in upper saloon.
L – Low bridge double deck with complete or partial sunken gangway in upper saloon.
B – Single deck.
DP – Dual purpose i.e. coach seating in bus shell or coach used for stage or express.
C – Coach.
Ch – Char-a-banc.
T – Toastrack.
O – Open top.
U – Utility specification.
F – Full front (on front engined chassis).
M – minibus.

After seating capacity:

C – Centre entrance.
D – Dual entrance.
F – Front entrance.
R – Rear entrance.
O – Open staircase.
FD – Front entrance with power door.
RD – Rear entrance with power door.
+29 – Standee with numbers of standing passengers.
8-8 feet width (Not used after 1956).
t – Toilet fitted.

Seating capacity:

Shown in figures. On double deckers, the upper deck is shown first (if known).
Examples: - H30/26RD would be a high bridge double decker with 30 seats upstairs, 26 seats downstairs with a rear entrance with doors.
B40D+29 would be a 40 seat single decker with dual entrance with 29 standee passengers allowed.

INTRODUCTION

The North Staffordshire area has not been the subject of a general view of road passenger service vehicles although the railway aspects have been covered in depth over the years. As far as buses go, the major work is the Transport Publishing book by Geoff Smith on PMT which came out in 1977. Small local books often give tempting fragments of bus history on a parochial level but except for books on Stevenson and Whieldon, the North Staffordshire scene has been neglected at the time of writing.

Over the years, fellow POPS members and I have collected photographs and it is from this pool of material that this very brief work has been collated. Many of these photographs are unattributed as the photographer is not identified. We owe a tremendous debt of gratitude to those who took the trouble to record the then current bus scene. In this book, I have used 'jargon' to appeal to the bus 'fan' whilst hoping that the general readership will also find something of interest.

Sadly, many of the older buses were unrecorded by photographers, or surviving 'snaps' are too poor to reproduce I hope, however that my selection will give a taste of one of the most fascinating English bus operating areas. I have drawn a line through Uttoxeter and Stafford as my southern boundary.

Unattributed photographs are from my own collection and I would like to thank fellow POPS members, Martyn Hearson, Thomas W.W. Knowles, Tim Machin, Graham Potts and Eric Wain for allowing me to delve into their albums for the treasure within. Also Chris Salmon has provided information on the more modern buses. Thanks to Bill Jackson for introducing the work to Mr. Trevor Berresford who kindly allowed me to use photographs from the Berresford family archive. The valuable help given by Mrs. Debbie Klemperer of the City Museum at Hanley, where the surviving PMT photograph collection is currently lodged is gratefully acknowledged. Thanks also to Dave Farrier, Robin Hannay, The Potteries Postcard Society, Geoff Smith and The Wessex Transport Society, for permission to use their photographs. My daughter and grandson, Jayne and Jack Tomkinson, both POPS members, have helped me to operate my ancient computer and my long-suffering wife, Eileen has now retrieved her dining room.

The vehicle details would have been impossible to record but for the work done by the Omnibus Society and PSV Circle whose permission to use is also gratefully acknowledged.

Finally I would never have started this work without the help and encouragement of an old friend and former colleague at PMT Head Office. Terry Moors managed to steer me through the maze of authorship whilst working on two of his own railway books. He also liaised with The Horizon Press on my behalf and let me use some of his photographs. I owe him a huge debt.

With over eighty operators involved in the early days between Tunstall and Longton and over one hundred and eighty operators coming to PMT either directly or indirectly, over the years, it is not possible to treat this modest work as a history. I hope, however, that the reader will savour a small taste of the transport oatcake that is North Staffordshire.

John Cooke, Lightwood

GLOSSARY

ABC – Associated Bus Companies Limited.

ABP – Associated North Staffs Motor Bus Proprietors.

AEC – Associated Equipment Company. Omnibus manufacturer of Southall, Middx.

ALL – As in all-Leyland. Chassis and body made by same maker.

Alliance – Group of local operators, including PET, not in the Associated group.

Association – Group of local operators including ABC who had a common fares policy and co-ordinated timetables. (Displayed on slip boards)

ATOC – Associated Trentham Omnibus Company Ltd. Ten operators who worked Stoke to Trentham on a rota basis.

BET – British Electric Traction Co. Ltd.

'Big Five'- Mainwaring Brothers (Absorbed 3rd June 1951), Brown's Motors, Milton Bus Services, Stoke Motors and Thomas Tilstone (All absorbed 10th March 1952).

BMO yard - Former Fenton Gas Works, used for parking BMMO buses in WWII.

BMMO – Birmingham and Midland Motor Omnibus Co. Ltd, ('Midland Red').

Charabanc - 'chara' for short is the anglicised version of the French term char-a-banc. It is literally cart with benches. The plural is chars-a-banc.

Dumb irons – front part of bus chassis frame. An identifying feature in earlier buses.

ECOC – Eastern Counties Omnibus Company

ECW – Bus body builder in Lowestoft descended from ECOC.

GBS – Green Bus Service of Uttoxeter (Whieldon's)

H&D – Hants and Dorset, a Tilling Group operator later part of the NBC.

Highbridge – A double deck bus with a centre gangway upstairs built to a height of 14ft.6ins.

Lorry-bus – After the end of WWI, 'demobbed' WD lorries were used as omnibuses.

Lowbridge – A double deck bus with a side gangway upstairs, total or partial built to a height, usually, of 13ft.6ins.

LTE – London Transport Executive. It was the administrator of LT.

MBS – Milton Bus Services.

MCW – Metro-Cammell Weymann. A bus body builder formed from Weymann of Addlestone and Metro-Cammell of Birmingham.

MCCW – Metropolitan-Cammell Carriage and Wagon. It was a marketing organisation for Metro-Cammell and Weymann's bodyworks.

MIRA – Motor Industry Research Association testing ground near Nuneaton.

MOS – Ministry of Supply.

MOWT – Ministry of War Transport.

NBC – National Bus Company.

NCB – National Coal Board.

NCB – Northern Coachbuilders.

NCME – Northern Counties Motor Engineering of Wigan.

NGT – Northern General Transport.

NSTC – North Staffordshire Tramways Company.

NWRCC – North Western Road Car Company.

OMO – One man operation. No conductor was used.

PET – Potteries Electric Traction Company.

PMT – Potteries Motor Traction Company.

POPS – Potteries Omnibus Preservation Society.

ROF – Royal Ordnance Factory.

Roundel – 'PMT' in a circle during the war to replace 'Potteries' which contravened the Defence of The Realm Act in that it indicated an area by name.

SEAS – Saunders Engineering And Shipbuilding of Beaumaris.

Short – Aircraft and Bus body builders.

SMT – Scottish Motor Traction.

SOS – Bus chassis built by Midland Red from 1924 to 1945. Thought to stand for 'Shire's Own Specification' after the Chief Engineer of Midland Red.

T&GWU – Transport and General Workers Union

Torque converter – Fluid coupling instead of a plate clutch.

TSM – Tilling-Stevens Motors.

'Unfrozen' – In 1940, bus production was 'frozen' to concentrate on military vehicles. Due to the extreme shortage of buses for the war effort, parts in store were later 'unfrozen' to ease the situation prior to new 'utility' production which began in 1942.

'Utility' – Wartime restrictions to save strategic commodities like aluminium were introduced. The MOS formulated a bus body design which eliminated curved panels, and used wooden seats and frames.

WD – War Department 1914. It impressed buses and drivers to serve with the Army.

WNOC – Western National Omnibus Company.

Chapter 1

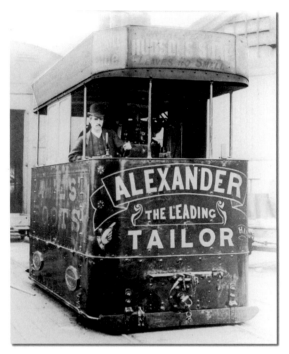

In 1879, the Hanley and Burslem Horse Tramway, a direct descendant of the 1862 Staffordshire Potteries Street Railway, was acquired by the North Staffordshire Tramways Company. The intention was to mechanise with steam engines and trailer cars. The first route was Stoke to Longton in 1880 with the horse tramway between Hanley and Burslem being converted soon after. The first engines were not successful and were withdrawn for a year before a new, improved 'Wilkinson type' engine built by Beyer-Peacock came into service. There were twenty of this class and the system was extended. Note that 'all-over' adverts are not a new idea on public transport. The NSTC trams ran on standard gauge track. *(PET/PMT)*

Believed to be a valedictory portrait of the end of the steam trams at Stoke, this photograph shows the staff in front of one of the locomotives which were numbered 1 to 20. The average annual figures for 1896 to 1898, the period of BET control over the NSTC showed almost four million passengers carried on over 360,000 car miles on 6.75 miles of route with receipts of 1/2d farthing per car mile. Not bad for just twenty locos and trailers, the later being bogie single deckers. *(PET/PMT)*

When steam finished, the trams were stored in a temporary 'graveyard' at Hanley Park, Shelton. The locomotives were sold for further use but the trailers, seen centre and right, were broken up. The new electric system was to a sub-standard gauge of four feet so they could not be used by the fledgling PET. The NSTC did not die, the tram conductors were employed by them and wore a distinctive hat as seen on the man fifth from the right. In fact the dormant company was still in existence in the nineteen forties. *(PET/PMT)*

PET Car 64 was new in 1900. It was built by the Electric Railway and Tramway Carriage Works whose 24-seat body was mounted on a Brill 21E truck. In 1902, it was rebuilt and lengthened to 36 ft 10 ins. as a 'combination car' mounted on Brill 22E bogies. The saloon seating capacity was thus raised to 46. The conductor is wearing the uniform of the NSTC formed in 1879, it used pillbox hats. The dormant company remained in BET ownership till after World War II. *(PET/PMT)*

1904 saw the introduction of The Motor Car Act. This meant that all mechanically propelled vehicles had to be registered with their local authority. PET had been chosen as a 'guinea pig' by the BET to trial a pair of Straker steam buses in 1900. These were not successful and had been withdrawn by 1904. The first motor bus was a Brush double decker, EH 30, later EH1. It was red and white with gold line with the name and crest on the sides and back. It weighed 3 tons 16 cwts. and was registered on 9th November 1904, its Brush body was O18/14F. The front wheels were 30 ins., the rear 42 ins. The registration EH1 was re-issued on the 3rd. August 1918 as a tower wagon (No.3) on a different chassis. *(PET/PMT)*

This early motor bus is almost certainly EH 2 registered on 29th. April 1905 under the 'Heavy Motor Car Act'. It is described as a '25H.P. Motor Omnibus, to PET- Top seated omnibus, red and cream panels, u.w. 3 tons 14 cwts. Axle loading:-front 1 ton 6 cwts., rear 2 tons 8 cwts., wheels 32'. It was cancelled on 23rd September 1918. It is clearly not a Brush like EH 30 and also differs in many respects to EH 4. A fourth 'primeval' motor bus chassis also carries EH 1 as a tower wagon (No.3) and that is different to all the others. Thus at least four different chassis were in use between 1904 and 1913. *(PET/PMT)*

EH4 was a 1905 Mutel with a T23 body. It had originally been a 'Top seated omnibus'. Its engine was also built by the French Mutel company. It is seen in this poor but unique photograph at the Commercial Inn, London Road, Stoke about to take some intrepid regulars of the pub on a trip. The 'Toastrack' preceded the more usual char-a-banc layout. This chassis was used as a basis for a tower wagon on 24th. June 1919. This was then transferred to a younger chassis and EH4 was sold by PET as a chassis to Brearley Garage, Marsh Street, Hanley. In November 1919, this amazing veteran was sold to Mr. Keats of Burslem for further use as a lorry.

Tower wagon No.3 is seen in King Street, Fenton outside Eagle's butchers shop, close to Fenton Depot, mounted on EH1. This chassis is different to the previous Mutel EH4 or the Brush EH1 (ex EH30) and at the time of writing is still unidentified. It is known that it was converted to tower wagon no.3 on 3rd August 1918. This tower was transferred to an unidentified Tilling-Stevens in the early twenties. The photo appeared in the PMT House Magazine courtesy of the late Charlie Smith.

The PET received their first 'modern' buses in 1913 and No.2, EH492 was a Daimler 'CD'/ Brush B31R. In 1915, the entire fleet was commandeered by the WD for active service. Luckily, they all returned unscathed and No. 2 is seen after 'demob' at an unknown location. The absence of destination boards implies that it was on a private hire. After receiving pneumatic tyres sometime in 1925, this grand old stager was withdrawn on 31st.May 1930 and was sold on 12th.November 1930 to a showman. *(Potteries Postcard Society)*

In 1920, Mr. F. Proctor began his business from Ravens Lane, Bignall End, with this Vulcan 'VSG' char-a-banc, EH 1776. Although licensed as a Ch18, there are twenty one persons visible. The driver, possibly Mr Proctor himself, has a passenger on his right but hand signals were not too important when the maximum legal speed was 12 mph. The lack of bonnet side panels implies that Vulcans ran hot! *(The late Albert Lawton collection via PMT House Magazine)*

PET photographic plate No.11 shows EH 1860, a Tilling-Stevens TS3 posed at Fenton Depot in 1921 in green liv-ery. It was an ex-W.D. chassis purchased by BMMO who immediately sold it, in 1920, to PET who mounted a Jack-son, of Sandbach, B28R body on it. It received fleet number 17 and was resold to BMMO in 1923 who rebodied it and re-registered it O 9931 until its withdrawal in 1928. The small plate above the number plate states the obvious- 'Hackney Carriage'. It carries a destination board for tram feeder short 'Hanford Bdge-Trentham'. *(PET/PMT)*

In 1919, BMMO acquired several Tilling-Stevens TS3 petrol-electrics in lorry form from the WD. Some ran as lorry-buses but most received Brush B29F bodies for themselves and sister companies of which PET was one. This was one of eight sent to Stoke in 1920 but they were soon withdrawn and returned to BMMO in 1923. It is posed in Bowstead Street. The etched ventilator glasses advertised the famous Hanley store of McIlroy's. The TSMs were not as reliable as Daimlers or Leylands and did not go abroad when in WD service as a rule. *(PET/PMT)*

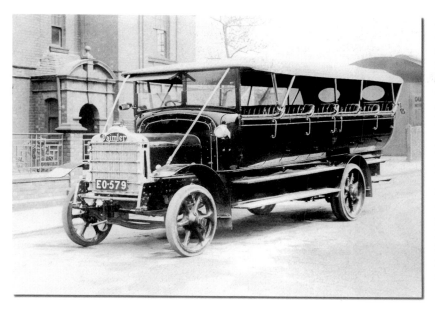

After the W.D commandeered all the PET buses in 1915, the BET was forced to fill the gaps. This Daimler CD with a Ch24 body of unknown make was one of a pair. EO 579 became PET No. 5 and was new in 1914 to Barrow who sold it on to Sheerness Tramways, both being BET subsidiaries. Both buses were withdrawn in 1929, No. 5 last running on 2nd.May 1929. Its body was sold to a Mr. Parrot on 29th.April 1930, its chassis being scrapped on the 15th.September 1930. *(PET/PMT)*

Chapter 2

'Old Bill Omnibus Service' was started in 1920 by Mrs S.E. Keeling operating from the Smithfield Hotel at Blythe Bridge. She was later joined by her son and in 1930 moved to Brook House. The 'Old Bill 'garage is today (2009), the terminus of First Potteries 6A to Biddulph. All-Leyland A5/B20F E 7033 was new in 1922 and lasted till 1925, when it was sold to Moreton, working on the Longton to Cheadle via Weston Coyney route. Later, licences were obtained for Longton to Caverswall and Dilhorne. Keelings were bought out by PET on the 1st. November 1932.
(Graham Potts collection)

Mr. J. Lymer started a service between Blythe Bridge and Longton in October 1923. This covered the Longton to Meir Road tramway but in February 1925, he changed to run to Hilderstone via Meir Heath which ran south from the Kings Arms at Meir. Outside the Smithfield at Blythe Bridge, where the bus was kept, is EH 6436, a Guy BB with B25F body of unknown manufacture carrying its 'Hilderstone' route board. The firm became a family partnership by 1931 and was taken over by PMT on 13th May 1939. *(Eric Wain collection)*

'Chara' trips were often segregated, men going one day and the ladies going another. A typical scene outside a hostelry sees a pair of chars-a-banc about to depart. The little Garford/Birch Ch20, EH 3637, new in 1922 was withdrawn on 11th. June 1931. It contrasts with the much bigger ex-WD Daimler 'Y' type. The American Garford was the first PET vehicle to run on pneumatic tyres. Two new ones were joined by another from Midland Red later. The little man in the white slop is Jess Redfern, who often acted as a courier on private hires in the twenties. *(PET/PMT)*

The Cooke, Robinson 1921 twins, Nos. 9 and 10, EH 3163/4 all-Leyland A7/ B18F are posed with two crews and what could be the proprietors. The firm grew to a moderate size in the late twenties and marketed themselves as 'The Incomparable Red Fleet' by means of postcards showing the fleet lined up. *(Graham Potts collection)*

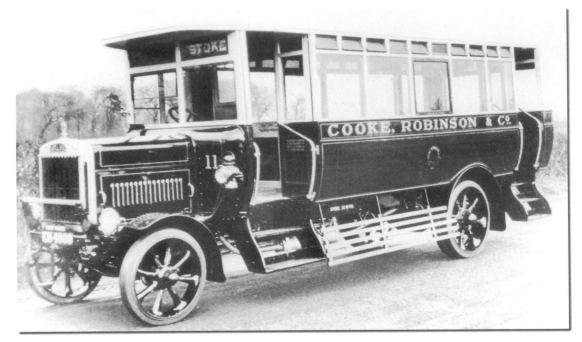

After the 'War to end all wars' Leyland bought back hundreds of surplus chassis, usually from the fledgling Royal Air Force. They were known as the 'RAF Type' or 'Reconditioned subsidy' and Cooke, Robinson availed themselves of a pair in December 1923. No.11, EH 4800 had a Leyland B30D body and lasted until sale in January 1927. Note that the speed, on solid tyres, was a bumpy 12 m.p.h. The registration plate bears the legend 'Hackney Carriage' above the characters. *(Graham Potts collection)*

Mr Bill Stonier Snr. purchased his fourth bus on 17th December 1924. EH 5968 was an all-Leyland C7 /B26R. The chassis cost £760 and the body cost £360. It only lasted until November 1927 when it was converted into a lorry. Probably an accident victim as sister C7, EH 7010 was sold on to Mainwarings at Bignall End in 1929 for further service. *(Tim Machin collection)*

Posed by the Queen's Park is PET Daimler 'Y' type/Birch Ch28, No.30. EH 3228, was new in 1922, the chassis being ex-WD. It was rebodied with a saloon body in 1927 before withdrawal on 30th June 1930 by which time it would have been converted to pneumatic tyres. The chassis was sent to the Birmingham breakers, Midland Motors, its new body being sold to NWRCC. This was the terminus of the tramway branch from Longton to Dresden; the last pole can be seen over the folded hood. Permission was not granted to extend this line to Trentham. *(PET/PMT)*

Intrepid passengers have paid 2/6d for a ride to Buxton on this 1913 Halley 28/34HP char-a-banc, EH 444. It was green and could be used as a goods vehicle as well as passenger. New to Harris Motors in Stoke, it is seen with Porter and Co., Bath Street, Leek. Many early buses had interchangeable bodies for freight or other purposes. Some were only used for passengers at weekends. A trip to Buxton with its fearsome gradients and weather extremes would have been an adventure in the pioneering days of private hires and tours.

One of the older independents in North Staffordshire was Pritchards Garage Limited of London Road, Stoke who ran on Tunstall to Longton. The two Thornycrofts are seen before delivery. The author has no details at the time of writing other than they clearly have a dual door body. Thorneycroft built bodies at this time but they also utilised Vickers. J.E. Pritchard became part of ABC in 1933. *(Tim Machin collection)*

Driver Arthur Taylor stands with his little Lancia, EH 3084, of F. Procter of Hanley. It was new in 1921 to an unknown operator and was acquired in April 1923. It was withdrawn in May 1928. F. Procter and Company has outlasted the other two members of the joint operation of the 16 Hanley-Leek via Cheddleton, Berresford and PMT, starting in 1923 and still going strong in 2009.

The crew pose with E 9787, their little Lancia on the erstwhile Leek to Hanley via Cheddleton route which was started by Mr J.M.Berresford in 1919. The Lancia which had a Petty B20F body, was new in 1924, when PET and Procters were also sharing the route. The bus was withdrawn in January 1929. The present day 16 route still has Procter, First Potteries pulling out in September 2008, Copeland's Tours do the Sunday service. *(Berresford Archive)*

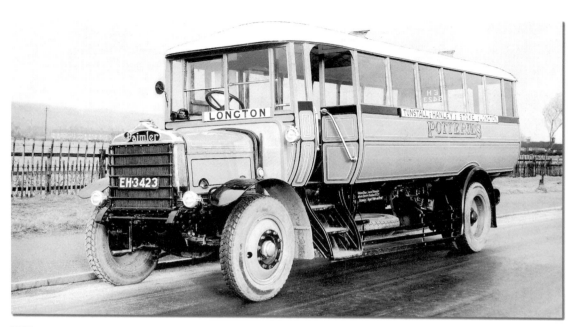

PET was among many operators to acquired former WD lorry chassis after The Great War. This Daimler 'Y' type was received in 1922. No. 19 has a Brush B29F body. The photograph was taken to mark the conversion of EH 3423 to pneumatic tyres in 1925. It carries destination boards for the Main Line and is posed in Campbell Road Stoke, near the old allotments, a favourite site until the thirties for official photographs for the company glass plate camera. *(PET/PMT)*

The interior of Daimler 'Y' type No. 19 shows the hide seating and the bell chord echoing the trams of the period. As an aside, the London Routemaster also had bell chords! The Brush B29F was later upseated to B31F, No. 19 carried Hackney Carriage plate No.103 and its engine number was Y151.It was withdrawn from service on 30th.June 1930 and was stored till 28th.April 1931 when it passed to Midland Motors (breaker) of Birmingham. *(PET/PMT)*

Mr. L. G. Wyndham Shire was the Chief Engineer of the Birmingham and Midland Motor Omnibus Company joining in 1912 when horses were replaced by motors. He was faced, in 1923, with the Tilling-Stevens petrol-electric chassis which was unreliable. He replaced the drive and electric motor with a dry clutch and four speed gearbox. The result was the SOS 'Standard' or 'S' type. PET took some early ones and No. 46, EH 4943. arrived in 1924 fitted with a Brush B31F body. It was loaned to Trent in July 1934 and returned on 28th September. It was then withdrawn and scrapped on 30th September 1934.

The early SOS 'S' types were licensed as Tilling-Stevens as they were conversions. No.44, EH 4941 is posed in Campbell Road when new. Most early BET saloons had Brush of Loughborough bodies as the two concerns shared a Director. This bus ran until 30th July 1935, a very creditable length of service for that time. The chassis was scrapped and the body was sold to a Mr. Gimbert of Meir Heath. *(PET/PMT)*

North Stafford Motors was started by Mr. F. Peake from 26, Stanley Street, Tunstall in August 1924. No.1 in his fleet was this little all-Leyland A13/B26F. It only lasted one month as it was the 'A13' demonstrator returning to Leyland after being registered by Mr. Peake as EH 5684. It was rebodied by Leyland in 1925 and was sold to Keighley Brothers of the eponymous town. They sold out in 1928 to West Yorkshire who withdrew it in 1930. North Stafford ran on the 'Main Line' as well as Hanley to Crewe, Tunstall to Mow Cop and Tunstall to Sandbach. They joined ABC in May 1939 and Mr. Peake became a Director and later held a similar position with PMT after the 1944 merger. *(G. Potts collection)*

'Enterprise' was a partnership between Mr. F. Haywood and Mr. C.M.Dawson formed in 1924 to compete against the ailing PET trams between Newcastle and Tunstall. In 1925, the partners split and Mr. Dawson set up his 'Reliance' company. This little Dennis has a Lawton B20F and is either EH 5055 or EH 6094. After 1925, Haywood ran Hanley to Newcastle and was operated as a subsidiary by PET from 17th July 1929 till 1932. *(Graham Potts collection)*

Car No.50 had a body by The Electric Railway and Carriage Works on a Brill 21E truck and dated from 1900. It was selected, with No.56, to be an experimental front exit car with the addition of vestibules. These two and the last tram, No.125, were the only PET cars to have windscreens. Seen when outshopped on 8th. November 1925, No.50 also says 'Please have fare ready'. This was a driver-only car and it worked on the Longton to Adderley Green route up Anchor Road. There is another photograph of this car with 'Front Entrance' on a sign, taken at the other end. Presumably this sign was moved to the trailing end when the direction changed. *(PET/PMT)*

The second batch of bogie cars was led by No.86, whose body was by Brush on Brill 22E trucks. These large cars had a capacity for 40 passengers. The author believes this to be between Hanley and Etruria during the General Strike when buses and trams, like the trains, had a police escort. At night, trams had a coloured light to signify the route.

Something went bump in the night! The Daimler bus, EH 8071, a B32F as yet to be identified, has collided with either Car 18 or 19. The latter cars started life in 1898, as trailers, numbered 18 to 27. The whole batch, built by Brush, soon went into store. In 1907, Nos.18 and19 were placed on new frames and they had a new compartment grafted on to each end. These made room for 44 passengers in a car that was over 38 feet long. Other rebuilds in this batch entailed fusing two complete trailers together to make a huge car over 40 feet long. *(PET/PMT)*

Mr. Jonathon Thomas Baxter commenced service from Broom Street, Hanley in 1922 with a bus on the Stoke to Trentham route. In January 1926, he bought this 1924 all-Leyland C9/B26D, MB 7226 from T. Biddulph, Dean Henshaw. It was withdrawn in June 1927 by which time Mr. Baxter had formed a partnership with L and C. Buckley on the 'Main Line'. In 1929, a Limited Company was formed and Baxter of Hanley was acquired by PMT in 1958. Baxter was one of the 'Alliance' group of PMT allies. *(The late Albert Lawton collection)*

Posed for the cover of the 1927 timetable at Wolstanton Marsh are Car No.82, a 1900 Midland Carriage and Wagon Company 40 seater on Brill bogies and SOS 'FS' No.88, EH 7901 fitted with a Brush B34F body. No.82 was sold at the end of operations in 1928 to Wemyss Traction who ran it until 1933. No. 88 was one of a pair new in 1926 and rare, as the Potteries Company were the only BET operator to acquire the 'FS' from BMMO. They hired another two from the manufacturer then bought them. The four lasted until 31st.October 1935 .They were sold for scrap on 30th.January 1936. *(PET/PMT)*

Baxter's fifth bus was this Leyland LSC1 Lion with unknown B31F body, new in 1926. EH 9855 is en route to Trentham. It was later sold to a Welsh operator who ran it until 1939.Note the legal lettering on the offside behind the driver's door. The Lion was sold in large numbers and was developed until 1939. It led to the famous TS1 Tiger which evolved until 1954 as the PS2 Tiger.

The business of G. Adams and Son was bought by Stanier of Newchapel in June 1930. This little Dennis, RF 1120 had gone by that time and nothing has yet come to the writer's attention about who made the B20F body which was new in 1925. Adams was one of several small operators who ran in the Mow Cop area with the 'Big Boys' like Stanier and Rowbotham. *(Graham Potts collection)*

The City Motor service was the trading name of O.W. Gurney of Shelton. Their base was adjacent to Shelton Church. Legend has it that an early chassis, perhaps this one, lies buried in the floor of the building, which still stands. EH 6912 was a Daimler 'Y' type fitted with a dual entrance body of unknown manufacture. It proudly sits on its Michelin pneumatic tyres in front of a most un-Potteries area three story terrace, so one concludes that it is a manufacturer's shot taken before delivery. Gurney ran Hanley to Longton via Heron Cross and was taken over by Tilstone and Stoke Motors in 1947. *(Graham Potts collection)*

Stafford Street in Hanley was the terminus for, amongst others, the Milton area group of services. Prior to August 1932 when his firm was taken over by the expanding Milton Bus Service, this neat little De Dion, RF 4291 ran from its home village of Baddeley Green under the control of Mr. J .Mayer who is seen with his conductor. He had the Stockton Brook route and also a hospital service. *(Graham Potts collection)*

Mr. Allen commenced running from Hanley to Smallthorne from his Sneyd Green base in 1921. He later formed a partnership with other members of his family and the route extended to the Riley Arms. In 1931, M.E. Allen and Sons, trading as Greyhound Motors purchased this Tilling-Stevens B10A2/Lawton B32F. VT 6211 is seen with its 'Alliance' board. Greyhound was acquired by PMT on 24th February 1935 and the bus became No. 250. It was re-numbered 10 before being sold to Beech the dealer on 30th November 1938.It passed to Stevenson, Spath who scrapped it in 1944. *(Graham Potts collection)*

A new PET Brush B37F bodied SOS 'QL' is seen at Stoke in 1928. One of fifty for tram replacement, it lasted until 1938. On the right is the original bus shed, the buildings behind are the tram shed. The whole site became Stoke No. 2 garage and Central Works later and most still survives in 2009. The 'QL' introduced roller blinds, made from linen although side boards are still in use. The four cylinder petrol engine had to be swung by hand and great care had to be exercised to avoid broken bones – or worse! *(PET/PMT)*

The Longton terminus for the Caverswall service was by the Market building opposite the Post Office. Here, the smart driver poses with his 'Old Bill' Bristol 'B' fitted with a, probably, Lawton B32F body. This bus was new to Keeling in 1928 and passed into the PET fleet as No.8. It was withdrawn on 25th August 1934 and three days later was sold to Beech the Hanley dealer. RF 4982 was of a chassis type which was not too common in the area until the arrival of the National Bus Company in 1969. *(Graham Potts collection)*

One of the subsidiary companies operated under PET ownership was W. Proctor & Co. Ltd. between 16th. May 1929 and 1932. They had acquired this Tilling-Stevens B9A from Cooke, Robinson in 1928. It was new in 1926, as a demonstrator. KM 1742 was known as 'Big 6' in the Proctor fleet and was allocated PET No.189. It was withdrawn on 16th May 1931 and on 27th May it was sold to a Birmingham scrap dealer. It is seen working the Longton to Cheadle via Tean service which came from Green and Aspey in 1928. Note the 'Association' board indicating a link with ABC as Proctor had a 'Main Line' licence.

Newly delivered to Thomas Tilstone is 1927 Tilling-Stevens B10A/Lawton B32F, EH 9136, Fleet No.4. It is noticeable that the maximum speed is still 12 mph. impossible to comply with even with a relatively primitive bus in 1927. The Lawton Motor Body Building Company supplied a canvas gaiter to prevent muddy spray. The bus was sold to Stevenson of Spath, who was fond of Potteries area buses, until they sold it as a lorry.

Berresford Motors acquired E.F. Milward of Cobridge, in March 1930 together with the Longton to Leek service and this Tilling-Stevens B10A/Lawton B32F. VT 2123 was new in 1928. When withdrawn it went to Gresswell of Billingborough for further service. Notable is the black on white destination seen on the bus at the Longton terminus by the Market Hall opposite the Post Office, a PET 'QL' is just visible round the corner. These termini in what is today, Transport Lane, were replaced by the new Bus Station in 1944.

North Stafford No.12, VT 5962 an all-Leyland LT2 Lion/B35F new 1931, is seen on trade plates before delivery. After joining ABC in 1939, it became No.9 in that fleet. On 20th April 1944 when the merger with PMT took place, it became No.509 but did not run for its new owner. On 23rd. September, it was sold to Leek Road dealer, Paddy Lewis for £170, clearly as a runner as he sold it on to Austin as their No.8. When they had finished with it, it passed to a showman. *(Graham Potts collection)*

This Guy FCB/ Fleming FB32F is believed to be VT 221 which was new in 1927 to Paul Prince of Burslem. He had been one of the founders of Stoke- on- Trent Motors in September 1925 working on Stoke to Newcastle with two buses. In April 1926, he withdrew to operate alone on the route. This service was acquired by PET on 26th April 1929 and a limited company was formed. Mr. Prince continued to operate tours and excursions until 1936 when this licence was taken over by PMT, the stage carriage licence having been taken over from the limited company by PET in July 1932. The Guy was numbered 38 and was withdrawn 30th June 1932 to Beech who sold it on to Grieg of Inverness. *(Graham Potts collection)*

Browns of Tunstall bought several new buses in 1931. No.1, VT 5754 was an all-Leyland LT2 Lion/B34F. The LT2 was in effect a TS3 Tiger with a four cylinder 5.1 litre petrol engine and a contemporaneous TD1 Titan radiator. Many operators in the area acquired this model and most lasted a long time in service. This one was withdrawn and sold to a showman at an unknown date probably at the end of the war.

This lovely photograph was given to Terry Moors by the licensee of the Brown Jug at Bishops Offley when he was on a publicity shoot for PMT in the eighties. In front is SOS 'QL' No.143, new 27th July 1928, withdrawn 31st December1937. It went to Beech (dealer) 26th.March 1938 and was with Williams of Buckhurst Hill by 1941. No.89 is one of only two SOS 'FS' types to come new to PET, on 15th June 1926. It was withdrawn on 31st October 1935 and went via Beech (on 30th January 1936), to Lewis for scrap. No.75 was one of the last SOS 'S' Standards, new 20th.April 1925.It was withdrawn 12th June 1935, its chassis going to Harper, Stoke, its body going to a Mr. Hassall of Tunstall. *(Terry Moors collection)*

The Leyland factory had a winner with the Tiger chassis which followed the highly successful Lion of 1928. The TS1, TS2 and TS3 versions were in production concurrently. This is Baxter of Hanley No.5, VT 6562, an all-Leyland TS1 Tiger/C32F new in July 1931. It displays its front wheel nut guard ring which was introduced earlier that year. The semi-floating rear axle lasted till the TS4 when a fully floating axle was used. In November 1943, it was rebodied with a Willowbrook UB34F and it lasted until October 1952.

A SOS 'QL' of 1928 poses, on 29th July 1930, in front of the PET Engineering Office on the corner of Woodhouse Street and Bowstead Street. The plate was made to show the advert for Mazawattee Tea an 'upmarket' brew. The bus shows also its Klaxon horn which had to be operated through the permanently open window. The petrol filler is also shown, the tank is under the driver's seat. The cab door hinges forward at the extreme front of the Brush body. Its capacity of 37 passengers is not far short of a modern Scania which is some twelve feet longer and 18" wider! *(PET/PMT)*

Cooke, Robinson of Hamil Road Burslem entered the ABC fold in March 1936. Prior to this, in 1932, they bought a trio of all-Leyland LT5 Lion/B35F saloons in their new lighter livery with the road safety triangle on the sides. They were Nos.1/3/6, VT 7471-3. They became ABC Nos.27/29/32. No.29 was scrapped in August 1940 but the other two were sold to Berresford Motors, as Nos. 10/1 in 1941. They were scrapped in March 1944 and September 1945 respectively. *(Tim Machin collection)*

No prizes for guessing who owned this bus. The largest single employer of labour in Stoke-on-Trent had a fleet of all sorts of vehicles to demonstrate its products. This all-Leyland TS1 Tiger/B32F, VT 5743, new on 3rd January 1931, was fitted with the new 'Real low pressure' tyres. In 1932, it was sold to Baxter of Hanley who ran it until 1937 when it was sold to Sutton of Knypersley. They withdrew it in 1944 after arduous service on their ROF services.

The story of the operators in the Audley area is very convoluted. The 'Mainwaring Brothers', were coal merchants and undertakers who also ran a bus. After several firms and even the PET Newcastle to Audley service were taken over, a partnership with T., E., W. and J. Mainwaring and Mr. F. Harrison was formed in the thirties. In 1951, as one of the 'Big Five', they were absorbed by PMT as they were not a limited company. Their garage at Bignall End became PMT Audley. Mainwaring Saloon RF 8823 was an all-Leyland LT3 Lion/B35F new in 1931. It became a lorry in January 1951. *(Tim Machin collection)*

C. S. Caswell, 115, High Street, Tunstall operated, in red, white and black livery, on Tunstall to Fegg Hayes. In December 1929, he became one of the earliest constituents of the ABC when he sold this route and a Leyland PLSC1 Lion to the new co-operative. His Main Line licence with this all-Leyland TS2 Tiger/B30F, No.3, VT 3341 and another two buses were bought by Tilstone in May 1933. No.3 became Tilstone No. 14 and was withdrawn and sold to Reid of Slamannon in December 1937. They scrapped it in August 1943. *(Tim Machin collection)*

Mr. J. Hawthorne commenced operations in 1919 in Fenton with a ten seat Studebaker but after several acquisitions, he moved to the Central Garage in Campbell Road, Stoke. His main service was Stoke to Trentham and the vehicles and licence for that route were sold to Associated Trentham Omnibus Company in 1932. He sold his remaining six buses, to PMT on August 12th 1934. This all-Leyland LT2 Lion/B30F is VT 6593 new in 1930 and sold to Beckett of Bucknall in 1933.It ran till 1938 before being passed on to a showman.

Rare indeed is this 1930 Sunbeam Pathan/B30F, its body maker is not known at the time of writing. VT 4796 was No.2 in the fleet of the Associated Trentham Omnibus Company. This company became a PMT subsidiary in 1934 the bus was absorbed into the PMT fleet, as No.8, in 1935. It was sold the same year to Ribblesdale of Blackburn. The photograph appeared in the PMT House Magazine thanks to the late Conductor Dennis Woodfint whose father was the proprietor of ATOC. Incidentally Dennis was named after the earlier bus in the fleet, a Dennis 'E' type. As can be seen, the 'Talkies' have arrived in Newcastle.

A line up of PET SOS 'M'/ Brush B34F saloons shows the next development after the 'QLs'. The 'Madams' were lowered and had racks inside for shopping to encourage ladies to use the bus. Also the smoking compartment that had been a feature of earlier buses was removed. Left to right are; – VT 2505/9/10/06/8, Nos. 156/160/161/157/159. The purpose of the photo is not known but No.159 has had its tyres painted white. No 160 appears to be in a different colour– green was used on some buses. Also No.159 is showing an 'ALLIANCE' slip board in the front window. 'M' class buses were new in 1929 and were gone by 1938. *(PET/PMT)*

Following on from the 'M' class from Midland Red was the SOS 'COD' saloon. These had a six cylinder engines and Brush B34F bodies. They were apparently to a specification for Trent drawn up by Mr. Clarke, their Chief Engineer. PET had a batch of twenty in 1930. Most were used as ambulances during the war and although No.216 was handed back, it was not used, being withdrawn in 1945. The driver contemplates the narrow cab of his 'COD' before taking it from The Ironmarket to Dimsdale in pre-war days. The company name was attached to the header tank.

Chapter 3

The first modern double decker in the Potteries, by less than one month was this all-Leyland TD2 Titan/L27/24R, VT 8363, No.14 in Fred Peake's North Stafford fleet. New in August 1932, it just preceded PET No. 27, a SOS 'REDD' which entered service 1st September 1932. No. 14 became No.5 in the ABC fleet in May 1939 and then PMT 505 in 1944. It was withdrawn on 31st January 1947 and was stored until being sold to Paddy Lewis on 16th December 1949 for £35. *(Graham Potts collection)*

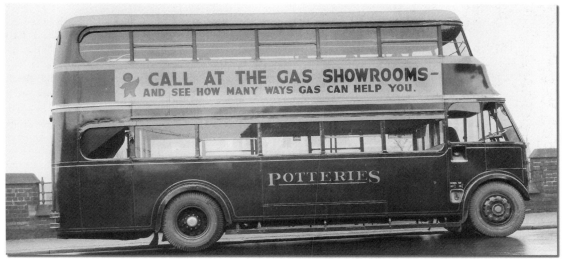

A damp and smoggy day before the war sees one of four SOS 'REDD' buses showing its advertisement whilst parked by the church wall in Bowstead Street. PET was the only operator of lowbridge 'Rear Entrance Double Deckers' bodied by Brush with this L26/26R of 1932. The characteristic 'piano front' can be clearly seen as can the petrol tap which is in the 'OFF' position. A swing of the handle and the engine would fire so taps were turned off when parked. The Klaxon horn is also seen with the glassless window. When ticking over, a SOS was silent, just a mild hiss from the carburettor to indicate that it was running. These rare classics ran until 1948/9. *(PMT)*

PET became PMT in 1933 when the company was reconstituted. The only new buses purchased in 1933 were five Leyland TD3 Titans. VT 9704 was No.26 and had a Brush L26/25R body with a 'piano front' of the then fashion. The indicator box is offset to allow for an advert to be placed on the nearside. The petrol header tank can be seen on the bulkhead. When the 1935 TS7 Tiger coaches came with oil engines they were exchanged with the petrol units in these Titans. No.26 was withdrawn on 30th November 1949 and sold on 27th February 1951 to Beresford, (dealer) Tunstall for £50. (PMT)

Mr. C.J. Whieldon was a driver for Stevenson at Spath when he decided to go his own way in 1927. He operated first from Hollington but by 1930 was running from premises in Uttoxeter. He changed his fleet name to 'Green Bus Service' and No. 9, AMB 833 was a Foden SDG6/Burlingham B32F which had been new in 1933 as a demonstrator. It was acquired by GBS in May 1934 and after being re-numbered 39 in 1949 was withdrawn in April 1953 to a showman. The long life of Fodens was well known and Whieldon's had many more over the years.

This futuristic machine is actually Green Bus Service No.11, ARE 489, an all- Foden SDG6 /C26C new in 1934. The retouched image suggests that Foden used it in advertisements at the time. During the war it was rebodied with an old Leyland double deck body then in 1946, it was rebodied again with a 1930 Massey L22/28R body from an ex-West Bromwich Corporation Dennis 'HS' double decker and it was withdrawn in November 1949.Its original body served as a family caravan before being used as a dwelling by a GBS driver.

Bearing a registration which today would be valuable, Mainwaring Brothers' No. 14, ARE 5 was a Maudslay ML3 with a Brush B36F body. It dates from 1934 and lasted until June 1940. The chassis was a rarity in North Staffordshire and one could speculate that spares may have been a problem, causing its withdrawal in the darkest days of the war.

The driver takes a break for his portrait at Wetley Rocks en route to Hanley. His Dennis 'EV', VT 4109 was new to Procter in January 1930. The body is not known, but has characteristics reminiscent of the Lawton factory. It was of B32F type. After withdrawal it passed to a showman like many old buses of the period.

Lymer of Tean bought this Dennis Lancet I/Willowbrook DP32F in 1933. It is seen at Alton Towers but it only ran until March 1936 when it was sold to Grainger of Ilkeston. It then passed to Barton transport until 1942 when they passed it on to Brown's of Donnington Wood who stuck with it till January 1950. Lymers passed their stage carriage services to PMT with some buses in 1939. They continued under the 'Victoria Tours' name as a coach firm until the eighties.

This postcard shows DEH721, a Bedford 'WTB'/ Willowbrook C25F new in 1936 to W.Jeffreys and Sons of Goldenhill. This charming little coach shows 'Sandbach' on its destination blind as Jeffreys ran on Thursdays to the famous Cheshire market. The 'WTB' was succeeded by the famous 'OB' model in 1939 and the latter was also bought by the firm after the war. *(Graham Potts collection)*

Berresford No.2, CRE 46, was a Dennis Lancet I/Willowbrook B32F new 1935. During the war it was upseated to B38F. In common with many buses in the fleet, it was long-lived being withdrawn in 1951. Note the sun roof and heavy coach style seats. Many single deck buses in the area were fitted for express services for industrial holidays. This is what later would be called dual-purpose (DP). The wartime extra seats could have been smaller 'bus' seats to allow for the legal clearances. *(Berresford archive)*

This 1935 PMT postcard shows No.222, BEH 951 a Leyland TS7 Tiger/Burlingham C32C. It came with the new 8.6 litre diesel engine which was immediately exchanged with a petrol unit out of the 1933 TD3s. Sometimes referred to as 'Coronation Coaches' the Tigers wore a variety of liveries including red, white and blue as well as all blue. They were the first vehicles to have 'PMT' as a fleet name. The coaches were re-engined again in 1951 with oil engines and they were withdrawn in 1952. No.222, on the 6th. May, was sold to Frank Cowley (dealer) for £80. He sold it to Blenkinsop of West Cornforth and by 1956 it was with a contractor, Boswell of Dudley *(PMT)*

Perhaps there were too many red buses in the area so Cooke, Robinson changed their livery to yellow and green, possibly when they became a Limited Company and moved to Hamil Road on the 7th June 1929. Here is Tilling-Stevens B10A EH 8986, No.3, new in March 1927, on withdrawal in 1930 to Kingfisher of Derby. Note the 'Alliance' board and the trade plates 019EH. Its battered 32 seat body bears the 'Safety' triangle and looks like a product of Lawton Bodyworks but this is not confirmed (in 2009)

Milton Bus Service purchased this all-Leyland LT7 Lion/B37F in 1935. No.7, CEH 26 was the latest Lion development. It had four cylinders so the engine was relatively short. This enabled the body to provide more space for passengers. The equivalent six-cylinder Tiger would usually hold thirty four passengers. MBS livery was usually two shades of brown, euphemistically called chocolate and brown, with a white roof. No.7 was sold, in 1942, to Richmond of Neath. *(Eric Wain collection)*

Davies of Hartshill bought No 2, DEH183 in 1936. It was an AEC Regal II/ Park Royal B36F. They ran it till it was sold to Beech, the Hanley dealer in 1951. They sold it on to Johnson of Allport who finally withdrew it in June 1956. The Mark II Regal had a four cylinder engine and so the bulkhead could be moved forward to give extra room in the saloon, hence the 36 seats. Note the interesting position for a destination board at the rear above the wheel.

Mr. H.T. Barker of Newcastle ran on Tunstall to Longton under the fleet name 'Dana'. His last bus was this 1935 all-Leyland TS7 Tiger/ B35F, CEH 182. In July 1939, 'Dana' was one of nine operators to become part of ABC, the bus becoming No.23. In 1944 when merged with PMT it became No.523. It was withdrawn on 31st December 1948. After the removal of major units, the hulk was sold, on 31st July 1950, to Beresford (scrap dealer), Tunstall for £20.

PMT 'went to town' to celebrate the Coronation of His Majesty King George VI. No.228, BEH 953 a 1935 Leyland TS7 Tiger/Burlingham C32C was filled with batteries to illuminate hundreds of light bulbs. The red, white and blue livery on this class of five led to their nickname of the 'Coronation Coaches'. This classic coach was re-converted to diesel in 1951 and was withdrawn on 30th April 1952 to Frank Cowley for £80. He sold it on to Banfield of London who ran it until September 1955 when it was scrapped. *(PMT)*

W. Tatton and Sons Ltd., mill owners, of Leek yielded their licences to Berresford Motors in April 1963. This 1931 all-Leyland Lion did not last that long and is seen wearing its delivery notices on its windows. The auto-vac tank for the petrol supply can be seen on the front bulkhead. The seating capacity is not known but was usually between 31 and 34 seats. *(Tim Machin collection)*

A classic thirties coach is exemplified by Associated No. 48, GVT 690 a Leyland TS8 Tiger/Willowbrook B37F new in 1939. This design progressed from 1934 to 1940 and was popular with independent operators all over the country. When ABC merged with PMT in 1944, No 48 became 548. Some of its sisters were refurbished by PMT and served as front line coaches. It was withdrawn on 31st December 1952 to Cowley who sold it to Stevens of Tredegar by March 1953 .They scrapped it in April 1955. *(Tim Machin collection)*

A 1939 shot of the terminus at Hanford (Church Lane) sees the 'one-off' PMT Daimler COG5/Weymann L30/26R No.120, FEH 840 new in 1938. Behind is a 1936 Leyland TD4 Titan. The streamlined No.120 was followed by a batch of very graceful Weymann bodied Daimlers of a different design. It became L136 in 1953 and was withdrawn in 1955 to Colbro (scrap dealer) of Rothwell.

This 1939 photograph shows PMT No.265, DVT 904, a 1936 Leyland TD4 Titan/Brush L30/26R in the Ironmarket. 56 seats in a lowbridge were more than the normal 53 at the time. It is standing at the 67 terminal which was a joint service with Reliance (C.M.Dawson) The bus stop flags in Newcastle were unique in the area , having the road safety triangle on top of the plate which contained the destinations. 'Bald' tyres were common in those days. The lining out in gold and the miniature 'Potteries' on the front would disappear during the war.

Chapter 4

Hazards of war! No. 156, GVT 121 was a Leyland TS8 Tiger new in 1939. Note the white paint on the wing, both types of headlight mask, the slit and the shade and the metal shade over the destination box. In 1951, her Brush B35F body went to Lewis for £5 whilst the chassis went to Beadle for the running units to form the basis of a new 'chassisless' vehicle, No.475, PEH 475 a Beadle FC35F8. This lasted, as C475, until 1958 when it was sold to PVD (Dunchurch) Many BET operators did this exercise on both Leyland and AEC chassis to give a modern looking coach pending the arrival of under-floor engined coaches in 1951/2. *(PMT)*

Sitting on the former tram terminus at Meir is SOS REDD No.236, AVT556. Its Short L30/26R body was laid bare by a lorry which came out of Meir Road and struck it as it was proceeding towards Longton. It is a miracle that there was no fire as the petrol header tank was in the middle of the carnage. The body can be seen to be camouflaged and a nice view of the PMT roundel, which replaced the 'POTTERIES' to confuse German parachutists, illustrates a fleet name only seen before on the 1935 Tiger coaches. Ready to tow the wreck to Stoke is former bus, lorry No.3, a 1925 SOS 'S' type formerly EH 6019. The date was 24th June 1943 and with another REDD war casualty, No 238, the pair were sold to Paddy Lewis for £60 after the war. *(PMT)*

Tilstone No. 5, BVT 72 was a late Leyland TS6 Tiger/Willowbrook DP37F new in 1935. Note the roof rack for cases and the deep leather seats. Willowbrook was a popular body maker for local independents and this design continued with style changes until 1940. No. 5 shows both types of headlight mask but no destination shade- bulb removal did the trick. She came to PMT but was sold on 9th April 1952 to Frank Cowley for £80.

(Graham Potts collection)

Ex-ABC No.73, HEH 817, was a 1939 Leyland TS 8 Tiger/ Willowbrook B37F and has received PMT fleet number 573 at the merger in 1944. Several buses were painted brown at this time due to a shortage of red pigment and this appears to be much darker than the usual shade. The PMT roundel is obscured by Frank Davies, the uncle of First Potteries Driver Bob Bentley who kindly supplied the photograph to the author. The bus was refurbished as a coach in 1947 and was withdrawn on 17th December 1952 to Cowley. It went on to serve Wimpey and another contractor.

The typical 'utility' bus of the war years was the rugged Guy Arab. PMT were allocated many of these stalwarts by the MOWT. The bodies, which had no curved panels, were single skinned, furnished with wooden seats, and usually built using unseasoned timber which resulted in them being rebodied or rebuilt in 1951/2. Here is Arab II/ Strachan UL 27/28R No. 336, JEH 569 when new on the new Longton Bus Station in 1944. It shows all the features expected and, like the ex ABC TS 8 on the next platform appears to be in brown livery. The Arab was rebodied in 1952 and became L267 being withdrawn in 1961 to Cowley who sold it on to Graham of Paisley.

(Graham Potts collection)

Almost vertical from a ditching at Spath, No.258, CVT 7 was a 1936 Leyland TD4 Titan with Brush L30/26R body. Note the camouflaged upper deck and the black painted windows–non transparent! It has white bumpers and wings. Not visible from this angle is the metal shade over the front box. No issues about hard hats then! The bus was withdrawn on 31st October 1950. In February, the body was scrapped 'on GM's instructions' and the chassis was sent for a new NCME H30/26RD8 body, becoming No.507. It was renumbered H67 and was withdrawn in 1954, its new body going to OPD2/1 Titan, NEH 452 to become H452. *(PMT)*

Also in trouble at Spath, No.260, CVT 9, lies in the foliage just up the road from No.258. Note that the rear number box has not been painted over with the green/brown camouflage. This Titan was the first of the ten in the batch to be withdrawn, on 31st December 1949. It was stored until its body was sold to Paddy Lewis for £15 on 20th July 1950. It went to Wigan for a new NCME H30/26RD8 and a new No.509. In 1953 it became H69 and it was withdrawn in 1954. Its new body was fitted to OPD2/1 Titan NEH 448 and the 'new bus' became H448. *(PMT)*

Very much a 'Flagship', No.222, BEH 951 was the first of the 1935 Leyland TS7 Tigers with the new diesel engines. The luxurious Burlingham C32C body was immortalised in glass over the Booking Office entrance in Church Street and as a drawing on the timetable cover long after withdrawal on 6th May 1952. On arrival, the engines were exchanged with the petrol units from the 1933 TD3 Titans. In 1945, it was filled with batteries to celebrate the end of the war. Its tyres have been whitened and it proudly shows off the new PMT badge in this view taken on Stoke City F.C. car park. A year before withdrawal, it was converted back to diesel power before going to Frank Cowley of Salford who sold it on to a contractor. *(PMT)*

Nearing the end of the road is Stevenson No. 9, VT4759, a 1930 Leyland LT2 Lion/ Lawton B34F new to Tilstone as No.3. It came to Spath in 1937 and survived until December 1953 a tribute to both Leyland and Lawton Bodyworks. Note that before 1950 nearside mirrors were not compulsory on buses.

The end of the war signalled an easing of the restrictions on body-building and in 1946, ten Guy Arab II/ N.C.M.E. H30/26Rs entered the fleet. They were still under the control of The Ministry of War Transport and, although they had curved panels in their design, they only had single skin panelling. No 346 became H293 in 1953 and they were all withdrawn to Cowley in 1960. They were the first 'High Bridge' buses delivered new to PMT so care had to be exercised in their allocation.

In 1935, PMT led the way with a large batch of Leyland TS 7 Tigers with three different bodies. These were among the very first quantity orders for the new Diesel engines, known as 'oilers'. The five which had coach bodies immediately exchanged them for the petrol units in the 1933 Leyland TD3 Titans. No. 83, the third from last had a Weymann B37F when new. In 1946 all, except one, were rebodied with new Brush B34F bodies like that seen on BEH 983. The exception had a double deck body after a fire in 1944. No.83 became S40 in 1953 and was withdrawn in 1955. Four lasted until 1957, almost a record length of service in the PMT fleet.

Austin of Woodseaves, later trading as 'Happy Days' operated this Leyland LT2 Lion with unknown B32F body. It was new in 1930 to J.E.Pritchard, Stoke who became part of ABC in November 1933, it becoming No.4. VT 4929 was then sold to Austin in 1940 as their No.25 running until March 1949, yet another tribute to the quality of Leyland buses and the teams of engineers who maintained them in running order for so long. This post-war view includes a Mulliner bodied Daimler of 1935 on the right.

Stoke Motors, one of the 'Big Five' were acquired in 1951 and operated as a PMT subsidiary company until 10th March 1952. No.9, FVT 81 was a 1938 Leyland TS8 Tiger/Willowbrook B37F which did not last long with its new owner being sold to Cowley of Salford for £80 on 2nd April 1952. He sold it on to Davies of Pontlottyn who ran it until 1954. Behind is a 1947 AEC Regal/Massey also of Stoke Motors. On the right, three Berresford buses load for Leek. *(Tim Machin collection)*

Proudly bearing its notice, at the City boundary at Goldenhill on 2nd April 1948, that it is No.5 in a new fleet of buses from Wigan, is PMT No. 369. LEH 749 was a Leyland PD2/1 Titan/ NCME L27/26R. It shows the lining out, in cream with fine black lines, which lasted until 1953 when all red was used as an economy measure.

No.369 became L341 in the 1953 scheme and spent most of its life at the little Goldenhill Depot. It was withdrawn in 1963 to Cowley who sold it for further use to Moordale of Newcastle on Tyne. They withdrew it for scrap in December 1965. This class of bus was one of the finest to serve PMT. *(PMT)*

'Rara Avis'! MV 346 was an AEC Ranger of Sutton Motor Services seen in Liverpool, probably on a private hire from Biddulph. Behind is one of eight ex- North Western Tilling-Stevens saloons which Suttons added to their large and varied fleet for operations to R.O.F. Swynnerton. They had a base in Stoke, taken over from Worthington's Tours in 1946, which was added to their Red Cross Garage at Knypersley and a garage in Kidsgrove. The petrol engined Ranger had a Park Royal C26R body and came from Scottish Motor Traction in 1941 having been a demonstrator.

No.10 in the Milton Bus Service fleet was NRF 950, a 1947 Leyland PS1/1 Tiger/Massey B35F. It came to PMT in 1951 and became S319 in 1953. It was withdrawn in 1960 to Frank Cowley. It was then split and chassis and body went to different scrap dealers. MBS had eleven PS1/1 Tigers with four different body manufacturers. Their livery was two shades of brown. *(Eric Wain collection)*

Stoke Motors had a share of the Hanley to Longton via Heron Cross service and No. 25, MEH 384 has just arrived at the Odeon. This is a Leyland PS1/1 Tiger with Massey C35F body complete with a roof rack for cases. It was new in 1948 and became SN373 in the PMT fleet. It was withdrawn in 1960 to Cowley who passed it on to a contractor for further use.

Just inside the north western corner of the area lies the village of Wrinehill. Contract and private hire services were provided by Sargent. One of their interesting vehicles was this Commer Commando/Plaxton C29F. HOA 543 was registered in Birmingham in 1948 and served Sargent in the early 60s. *(Graham Potts collection)*

O.W. Gurney operated from Shelton under the fleet name of 'City Motors' on the Longton-Heron Cross-Hanley route. In 1947 they were taken over by Stoke Motors and Tilstone, KVT 194 going to the former. It was a 1947 Leyland PS1/Willowbrook B35F. When acquired by PMT it was numbered S324. It was withdrawn in 1958 and its body was removed. Its chassis languished for some years alongside the PMT snow plough in Bowstead Street after being stripped for spares.

Mr. Ernest Wells commenced service in May 1914 with a Durham-Churchill char- a- banc. It and Mr Wells were commandeered by the WD and he spent the Great War trooping in the United Kingdom. After the war, he expanded using mainly Dennis buses. After acquiring the Hanley to Over service from Millward of Cobridge, a limited company was formed in October 1933. Two other firms were taken over until PMT acquired a controlling interest and ran Wells Motor Services Ltd. as a subsidiary from 1953 till March 1959. Typical of the fleet is this Dennis Lancet I Duple B38F. No.3. CRF 631 was bought in May 1934 and is seen in Tower Square, Tunstall. It lasted until July 1952 when it was scrapped. *(Graham Potts collection)*

Posed at Trentham Gardens in 1947 is No.572, HEH 816, a Leyland TS8 Tiger/Willowbrook C35F new to ABC in 1939 as a B37F saloon. After the 1944 merger, PMT found that several of these Tigers were sufficiently sound to be refurbished as coaches as 572 here shows. It was withdrawn on 17th.December 1952 to Frank Cowley for £135 and a £2/10/- delivery charge. He sold it to Carlton of Newbrough then later it went to Burrell of Ashton under Lyne. They disposed of it to Used Units of Burnley for scrap in 1958. *(PMT)*

Still showing a matt brown camouflage roof at its Scotia Road home is Brown's Motors No. 31, GVT 522. It was a 1939 AEC Regal/Duple B37F, one of three in the batch. During the PMT subsidiary period between May 1951 and February 1952, it was painted red and its fleet number became 31B until the 1953 re-numbering made it S185. It was withdrawn in 1957 to PVD (Dunchurch) who sold it on to Colbro a contractor who passed it to another contractor, Crouch, who withdrew it in January 1961. The quality of the Duple body is reflected in its longevity. *(Eric Wain collection)*

The old cottages in Stafford Street, Hanley form a background to Brown's Motors No. 57, KEH 7, a Daimler CWA6/Duple L27/28R new in 1946. This 'relaxed' utility was issued under the authority of the MOWT and its rigidly mounted AEC 7.7 litre engine will soon be banging its way to Talke Pits. The interior was still single-skinned but the seats are now upholstered and the rear dome is curved. The bus became L284 in 1953 and it was rebodied with a NCME L27/26R lightweight body in 1954, its old body going to Lewis of Leek Road. It was withdrawn in 1963 to Cowley and scrapped. *(Eric Wain collection)*

Problems at Leyland after the war led to many delays in the delivery of new buses. A batch of twenty high bridge buses to follow on from the 1947/8 low bridge Titans should have arrived at PMT in 1948/9 but all arrived in 1949. Nos.390-409, LEH 770-789 were Leyland PD2/1 Titans with NCME H30/26R bodies. They were the last new 7ft.6ins.wide double deckers in the PMT fleet. After spending most of their lives at Burslem and Newcastle Garages, they were all withdrawn in1964 to Cowley. Only three were sold to contractors for further use. *(PMT)*

Stoke Motors No.4, BVT 658 was a Leyland TS7 Tiger/Willowbrook DP37F new in 1935. Its roof mounted luggage rack will not be required on this imminent trip to Hanley via Heron Cross, a service shared with Tilstone, in the late forties. No.4 did not last long enough to receive a PMT fleet number in 1953 being withdrawn to Cowley who sold it on to Barton (Contractor) of Ainsdale. They sold it for scrap in April 1955. *(Eric Wain collection).*

The first buses of 1939 for PMT were five Daimler COG5/Brush L30/26Rs. Doyen of the class was No.41, GVT 101 seen here 'on the church wall' in Bowstead Street in the late forties. Its striped livery was a simplified version of the gorgeous pre-war gold lined vision which graced the fleet until the war put a stop to elegance for good. No. 41 stares at a Roe-bodied Guy Arab new in 1945 oblivious of its future career with Wimpey Building Contractors from 1952 to 1955 and oblivion.

When ABC merged with PMT in 1944, 500 was added to their fleet numbers. No. 543 was an early (1938) Leyland TS8 Tiger. In 1949, the old Willowbrook body on FEH 785 was replaced with this Weymann B35F. In 1953, the bus became SN121 and it was withdrawn in 1957 and went, via a dealer to Banfield Coaches in London S.E.17. It is in Hassall Street Bus Station in 1952. The new concrete shelters were erected to mark the new Elizabethan age, one still exists in 2009, not far from Newcastle. *(PMT)*

Chapter 5

The BET Federation designed standard bodies and parts for member company's fleets. In 1950, fifteen of the design came new to PMT. Nos. 431 to 444 were Leyland PS2/3 Tigers/Brush B34F8. Registered NEH 431-44, they were unique to PMT as they were eight feet wide. The 1953 renumbering scheme erroneously dubbed them 'SN'. This was altered to 'S' a few months later as, being without boots, they did not come to the 'SN' standard. They were withdrawn in 1962 to Cowley who sold the lot to various nationally known contractors. *(PMT)*

This is the interior of PMT No.450. It is a Weymann B35F8, one of twenty four to arrive at the end of 1949/early 1950 mounted on Leyland OPD2/1 Titan 'export' double decker chassis. The bulkhead heater, an innovation on a PMT saloon bus, is prominent and the luggage racks on each side were complemented with a boot. NEH 450 received the Northern Counties L27/26RD8 body from DVT 904, a 1936 TD4 Titan on 2nd March 1956 and it became L450. The Weymann body was fitted to ex-Tilstone PS1/1 Tiger S362 on 11th July 1957 becoming 'SN' for a short time. It was withdrawn as S362 to Cowley in September 1962. *(PMT)*

1938 Leyland TS8 Tiger No.150 was one of ten to be withdrawn on 31ˢᵗ.October 1949 for further use as coaches. The old body was sold for £5 to Lewis, the Leek Road scrap merchant and the chassis was driven to the Windover factory to receive this luxurious C33F8 body entering service in early 1950 being renumbered 499. It was further renumbered in 1953 as C116. On withdrawal in 1957, it passed via Colbro (dealer) of Rothwell, to Mercury of Boscombe who ran it until May 1959.This class marked the end of PMT half-cab coaches as the new underfloor engined vehicles were imminent. *(PMT)*

In 1950 PMT and other bus companies were still boasting that they were charging pre-war fares as well as being privately owned. The former was a mistake which could not have been foreseen, Suez in 1956 changed forever cheap fuel. Complete with its propaganda notice, newly rebodied No.490 undergoes its tilt test at Stoke under the control of the Matador. FEH 806 had been bus No.131, a Leyland TS8 Tiger new in 1938 its Brush body had been changed for this Windover C33F8 body. It became C98 in 1953 and was withdrawn in 1957 to PVD (Dunchurch) who sold it on to Lloyd of Nuneaton. After service with them it passed to Palmer Scaffolding who scrapped it in August 1962. *(PMT)*

Mainwaring's service from Newcastle to Butt Lane at Kidsgrove, via Talke Pits needed single deckers due to the low bridge at Chesterton. No.23, ORE 432 was one of a pair of Guy Arab III/ Burlingham B35Fs purchased in 1948. It ran un-numbered in 1951/2 becoming PMT S385 in 1953. It was withdrawn in 1960 to Cowley of Salford. The unique Newcastle bus stop flag with road safety triangle can be seen by No.23.

Tilstone No.27, JEH 67 was an 'Unfrozen' Bristol K5G whose Duple L27/28R body was to pre-war standard even though it was delivered on 1ˢᵗ. April 1942. The body was similar to a batch for Red and White and must have been stored at Duple until a chassis was found. It was painted red during the subsidiary period and was numbered T27 before being renumbered L232 in 1953. It was withdrawn in 1955 to PVD (Dunchurch). They sold it on to Chambers of St. Mary Cray.

'Badge Engineering' is seen on a 'one-off' Maudslay Marathon IV/ Gurney-Nutting of Kildare Street Garage (KSG.) owned by Mr. Need of Dresden. The author remembers well this vision in regal purple as it had tables and curtains-a rare sight in 1952! The Maudslay was an example of a large company(AEC.) getting an extra stand at the Commercial Motor Show at Earls Court as it was identical to the AEC Regal IV. Sadly, Mr. Need was ahead of himself as no-one, even football teams, could avail themselves of such luxury. The coach went to Bassett's Coach-ways and served for many years. The little garage still exists in 2009.

Queen's Gardens in the Ironmarket was the location of the Newcastle stand for the Chesterton and Audley areas. Mainwaring Brothers No.22, BRY 266 was a 1937 all-Leyland TD5c/H27/26R new as Leicester No. 304. It was acquired in 1950. Leicester had removed the torque converter and replaced the 6.8litre petrol engine with the 8.6 litre diesel which made it ideal for the hilly North Staffordshire terrain. Acquired in 1951, it became PMT H84 in 1953 and lasted until 1954 when it passed via PVD to Smith of Reading for further service.

Baxter (Hanley) Ltd. purchased this fine coach in February 1949. No.6, NVT 678 was a Leyland PS2/3 Tiger/Lawton C35F8 and was one of the last half cab bodies to be built by that fine local builder. It is seen outside the yard on the southern fringe of Hanley Deep Pit where today the Potteries Way passes about fifty feet below the camera. No.6 became PMT C504 in 1958 and was withdrawn in July 1963 as the last PMT half cab coach. It was painted at Stoke into a deep blue livery for the Staffordshire Police Central Sports Club. After they had finished with it, it was sold on to a contractor in Wolverhampton by July 1970. *(Tim Machin collection)*

The small but vigorous firm of Metalcraft was set up after the war in the former Finishing Hanger of Rootes Securities of Blythe Bridge at the southern edge of Meir aerodrome adjacent to Grindley Lane. They built just over one hundred mainly coach bodies. The most prolific were forty-one on Foden chassis. Typical of these is OEH 739 a Foden PVSC6/ Metalcraft FC33F new, in 1950, to A.H. Davey of Newcastle. One of the top bodybuilders at Metalcraft was the late Albert Lawton, who later became charge hand at the PMT Body Shop in Central Works. Albert was a noted historian and craftsman. The author is proud to have been a colleague during the time of the House Magazine when Albert was a regular contributor. *(Eric Wain collection)*

Potteries No.266, DVT 905 was a Leyland TD4 Titan new in 1936. In 1951, it was rebodied with this NCME L27/26RD8 body which featured air changing. Ten highbridge and five lowbridge buses were involved and this combination ran until 1955/6 when the pre-war chassis were scrapped. The bodies were fitted to 1949 Leyland OPD2/1 single deckers, this one becoming L455. L453 of the same batch is preserved and lives, at the time of writing in the Canvey Island Bus Museum.

During the Second World War, large numbers of 'Utility' double deckers were rushed into service with PMT. Most were the strong Guy Arab Mark I or II but all had basic bodies, by Strachan or Duple, usually with unseasoned wooden frames and all had wooden slatted seats. As their bodies were sub-standard, some were rebuilt but most were rebodied. In 1951 a newly rebodied, by NCME, Arab displays its footwear advert. These bodies had air changing in the upper saloon and nice leather seats. Most had a Gardner 5LW engine which struggled on hills but they all lasted until 1960. *(PMT)*

February 1952 marked the death of H.M. King George VI and a severe vehicle crisis at Stoke. Frank Cowley came to the rescue by selling a fleet of elderly, but serviceable double deckers to PMT. One of these is seen in Hill Street, Stoke waiting to go to Newcastle. ARU 166 is in green Hants and Dorset livery and is a 1935 Leyland TD4 Titan with Brush L26/26R body. Originally a TD4c with torque converter and petrol fuelled, it was converted to normal gearbox and oil fuel by H&D. It still has its fleet number plate (991) fitted. It was painted red by September 1952.

Seen after the 1953 numbering scheme, ARU 166 has become L11. The Stoke Bodyshop has also painted it red, changed the drop-windows for sliders and fitted a standard PMT destination box. The body repairs have included the 'trademark' of the Central Works the curved 'corners' to the lower deck windows. The observant will also have noted the singling of the upper deck hand-rails and the provision of a starting handle. The latter suggests an engine change although still the melodious 8.6 litre unit. It is about to leave Leek Cattle Market for Hanley. It was withdrawn in 1955.

In 1952 a batch of seven AEC Regents with Park Royal L26/26R bodies were bought by PMT from sister company City Of Oxford Motor Services. Numbers 124-130, HFC 414-420 were new in 1939 and became PMT L164-170 in 1953. As would be expected with vehicles from this immaculate fleet, nothing needed to be done to them before service. One is seen in 1952 showing off its 'Burton's Gold Medal Biscuits' advertisement. L167 was written off after a bad accident in 1955 and the others were withdrawn in 1956/7. *(PMT)*

GUP451 was a Foden PVFC5/SEAS B35F new in 1947. It was bought by Sutton in 1952, one of six, from Crown of Birtley. Saunders bodies were not as good as their aircraft which could explain why the bus appears to be at Lawton for refurbishment and still awaits its headlights. On takeover of Sutton by PMT in April 1955, this and four others went to Horseshoe of Kempston so the craftsmen at Lawton must have done their usual magic and extended their lives. Only the Newcastle to Congleton route was taken over by PMT, becoming No.74, the buses departed, nearly all, to local operators. *(Graham Potts collection)*

The vehicle crisis of 1951 was caused by the influx of elderly buses from the 'Big Five'. It was solved by PMT acquiring many old, but serviceable double deckers. L5, UF 9757, was a 1933 Leyland TD2 Titan/ Willowbrook L27/24R, one of three which came directly from Southdown. It was received on 12th November 1951 and entered service at Stoke Garage on 8th December 1951. It survived until 1954 by which time the crisis was over. Its longevity was helped by a new body in 1944 by which time the 'utility' regulations had eased a little.

Among the more modern buses acquired by PMT in 1952 from Frank Cowley were a batch of AEC Regents from Halifax Corporation. H151, JX 6429, takes a breather in Old Hall Street before a relief crew loads its Park Royal H30/26R body with returning residents of Abbey Hulton. The big 8.8 litre engine of these Regents was ideal for climbing the steep Limekiln Bank. They also had large circular heaters on the front bulkhead, a luxury in the Potteries area. H151 lasted until 1957 when it returned to Cowley.

Not all was 'gloom and doom' in 1951 as PMT were among the first to obtain new, very heavy, underfloor engined Leyland PSU1/15 Royal Tigers. They were fitted with the classic Burlingham 'Seagull' C39C8 bodies. PVT 15 arrived in early 1952 and became C515 in 1953. It was used by the Australian Cricket Team for their Tour and it was very specially 'bulled up' for the job. The door window also displays the Coronation motif which appeared on buses all over the country in June 1953. The company initials are displayed in polished aluminium, the only vehicles so treated. Royal Tigers were so heavy, and fast, that the brakes were hardly up to the job so most Seagulls had new faces before withdrawal in 1964. *(PMT)*

Blackfriars Tours of Newcastle bought this Maudslay Marathon III/Burlingham FC39F in 1951. PEH 360 was christened 'Billy' and the body was the variation of the classic 'Seagull' design for front-engined chassis. The heavy looking front end did nothing to improve the appearance and provided the driver with poor visibility to the nearside. *(Graham Potts collection)*

Stranger in camp at Woodhouse Street is all-Leyland PD2/3 Titan/H30/26R8, H487. OEH 887 was one of five of this classic, new in 1950. It is seen in 1954 outside the PMT Head Office. Allocated to Stoke it was usually to be found on the Longton to Meir via Chaplin Road, an old Stoke Motors working, care had to be exercised in getting to Longton as Highbridge buses had to go via Heron Cross and Longton Hall Road. It has half-drop windows, unusual at this time suggesting that it was a diverted order from South Africa. These fine buses were withdrawn in 1964.

Star of the 1952 Commercial Motor Show at Earls Court was the prototype Daimler CLG5/MCW 'Orion' H32/26R8, REH500. No.500 is seen with a load of journalists at the MIRA testing ground near Nuneaton, bouncing over the 'Belgian pavé'. The 'L' in its designation stood for 'Lightweight' and at six tons four hundredweights, it was lighter than most single deckers of the day. It acted as a demonstrator in 1953 after it was decapitated by Longton Station Bridge. It was repaired by Metro-Cammell and served out its days at Clough Street then latterly at Stoke on the 150 Penkhull Circular, until 1967 when it went for scrap to Cowley. *(PMT)*

Half cab buses are not easy to enter but once inside, the view is great. This is prototype Daimler No.500 when new showing its unique livery. The red has very fine gold lining out similar to the then current Midland Red style. In 1953, as H500 the bus was used as a demonstrator for a time notably for Manchester Corporation. The cab layout was unique in the PMT fleet as the starter switches were above the driver on the left. This is where London Transport located their starters. The control lever for the Wilson pre-selector gearbox was to the early style, moving in one plane. Later Daimler buses had the gear lever in a quadrant of 'H' format. *(PMT)*

A quiet day, Sunday or Thursday half-day closing sees Stonier No. 5, FVT 649 a Leyland TS8 Tiger/ Willowbrook B37F, new in May 1938, contemplating the shop blinds of McKnight's Gents Outfitters. This classic design was very popular with the independent operators in the area. No.5 is working the Meir via Bucknall route which Mr. W. Stonier Snr. started in 1930. The bus was withdrawn in June 1956 to Cowley.

It did not find a buyer so it was scrapped. *(Tim Machin collection)*

This fine photograph shows the Wolstanton (Silverdale Road) bus stop on a busy day with Newcastle bound intending passengers mostly standing in the road. So much for easy access! H525, REH 525 was an AEC Regent III/NCME H30/28R8 new in 1952, one of the batch which was the last to be delivered before the 1953 renumbering system. The recently applied 'H' shows nicely the date as being early 1953. PMT at this time still used sans serif characters for fleet numbers at the rear and serifs everywhere else. This superb bus was withdrawn in 1967 to Cowley for scrap. *(PMT)*

A dire vehicle shortage at PMT in 1952 caused the BET Board to step in and ten vehicles were diverted from a Northern General order. Six of the ten ran in NGT maroon and ivory livery, until their first repaint in 1955. Seen before delivery in October 1953, is one of the PMT red ones. H542, SVT942 was a Guy Arab IV/ Weymann 'Orion' H32/26R8. This class was the first to be delivered with the new fleet number system applied. They had a rear destination box which was eventually panelled over. H542 was withdrawn to Cowley at the end of 1966. *(PMT)*

The shipping difficulties in the dark days of 1940 resulted in many buses intended for export being allocated to British operators. A batch of eight intended for Salisbury, Southern Rhodesia were built in 1941. They were thirty feet long and eight feet wide. This meant that Parliamentary dispensation had to be given before they could run in the U.K. Seven came to PMT as Nos.294–300, where their huge bulk earned them the nickname 'Battleships'. HVT 816-22 were Daimler COG5/40/ Weymann B39F8. In 1950 they were rebuilt and re-registered OEH 294-300. In 1953 they were renumbered S213-19. Just after this, S217 displays its ample proportions and demonstrates its rear advertisements. They were all withdrawn to Cowley in 1959. *(PMT)*

The author wielded his Brownie at L227, AJA 195 a Guy Arab I/Roe UL 27/28R as it passed brand new Leyland PSUC1 Tiger Cub/Weymann 'Hermes' B44F8 S547, SVT 547, in January 1954. The Arab was new in 1942 to NWRCC and was swapped in 1947 becoming PMT No.581. It was withdrawn in 1955 to PVD (Dunchurch) who sold it to Millar (Contractor) of Edinburgh. S547 was withdrawn in July 1967 to Cowley (Dunchurch). Uniquely when new, the 'Cubs' had sans serif fleet numbers on the front. The bottle ovens and bus station at Longton are now covered by the Bennett Precinct shopping centre. *(Author)*

Another Brownie shot, this time on the parking area of the old Longton Bus Station. S220, HVT 919 was a very rare Leyland TS11 Tiger/ Willowbrook UB36F. Only twenty two of this 'Unfrozen' chassis were produced, PMT had two, Browns and Stoke Motors had one each. It was withdrawn in 1955, swapped registration numbers with S20, a 1935 TS7 Tiger, and went to Hulley of Baslow as BEH 963. The TS11 was a very advanced chassis which but for the war would have gone into full scale production. Leyland had to concentrate on tank and lorry production *(Author)*

The old Newcastle Bus Station plays host to L75, one of four 1937 Leyland TD4s from Hants and Dorset via Cowley of Salford. CRU 703 is much as built, its Brush L27/26R body retaining its half-drop windows and H&D destination box. Its newly applied 1953 fleet number shows up well on the sparkling red livery applied the previous summer. The long 46 to Blurton ran via Bradwell, Burslem, Hanley and Stoke. L75 was withdrawn in 1955 back to Cowley. *(Wessex Transport Society)*

Not what it seems is PMT L13, BEH 957 a 1935 Leyland TS7 Tiger whose original Brush B37F body caught fire in 1944. As the need was great for double deckers it was rebodied by Burlingham with this L27/26R to their pre-war design. The chassis was upgraded to the equivalent of the TD5 Titan. It was renumbered from 57 in 1953 and is seen in 1955 just before withdrawal at Stoke. Note the pre-war 'split' blind from a single decker. *(Geoff Smith)*

PMT opened its Hanley Garage at Clough Street on 27th February 1953. It was built on former colliery spoil tips, some of which can be seen to the left. Ex-Brown's Motors Daimler CWA6, No.60, KEH 269, became L286 in 1953 and its Duple relaxed utility body was replaced by this lightweight NCME L27/26R in August 1954. It was fitted with Hanley Garage 5/6 destination blinds for its Certificate of Fitness portrait on 30th August. It returned to Burslem where it served until 1963 when it went to Cowley who passed it to a Barnsley scrapman. *(PMT)*

This picture was one of a series to feature the new 'Essex' bus washer at Stoke Garage on 11th.March 1954. It shows C100, a Leyland TS8 Tiger/Windover C33F8 coach about to be washed. Of more interest in the background, is part of the extensive programme of body swapping which PMT did in 1954. The Leyland OPD2/1 Titan/Weymann B35F8 bodies are being lifted prior to fitting to older chassis. A remarkable coincidence sees the chassis of NEH 466 on the left and its Weymann body about to be fitted to Guy Arab II ex MBS No.3, (S333) MRF 350. The OPD2/1 will return from NCME as L466 and in 1977, it will become the 'Flagship' of POPS. *(PMT)*

A repaired panel which needed to be repainted does not have to be fixed in the Paint Shop at PMT Central Works. Garages could use a simple heating rig like this to dry the new paint. H65, CVT 5 was a Leyland TD4 Titan new as No.256 in 1936 with a Brush L30/26R body. This body was transferred to TD5 No.249 (later L80) in 1951 and this new NCME H30/26RD8 body was mounted on the 24th March 1951. CVT 5 was renumbered 505, becoming H65 in 1953. On 20th October 1954, this body was put onto OPD2/1 Titan NEH 457 becoming H457 and CVT 5's chassis went to Cowley for scrap. (PMT)

Seen at Trentham Gardens showing off its smart new livery in 1955 is H445. NEH 445 was a 1949 Leyland OPD2/1 Titan which was delivered to PMT on 9th January 1950 carrying a Weymann B35F8 body. On 30th September 1955 it received this 1951 Northern Counties H30/26RD8 body from 1936 Leyland TD4, CVT 3 whose chassis was scrapped. Its Weymann body was fitted to S372, a Leyland PS1 Tiger ex-MBS. H445 was withdrawn on 4th.February 1965 to Frank Cowley. The cream roof did not stand up well to the local atmospherics so after 1959, the upper deck was painted red. *(PMT)*

Green Bus No. 22, XRE 978 was specially built by Guy Motors for the company. It was a Guy Arab III with B35F body new in May 1952. It was the last standard single deck Arab III and one of the last half cab buses built new in the country. The chassis was made up from existing parts at Wolverhampton. The engine was supplied by Green Bus and the body was a surplus one held in store at the factory. It lasted until September 1965 when it was used for spares until being sold for scrap to Burns of Brereton in May 1966. *(Robin Hannay)*

The Author's trusty box Brownie caught Baxter No. 15, NV5141 in Longton Bus Station just before it was sold on to an operator in Essex. It was a Leyland TD4 Titan/ ECOC L27/26R new 1935, acquired from United Counties in 1952. Its twentieth year saw this sturdy bus return to Blackwell of Earls Colne. Baxter's livery was red and ivory with a maroon roof and as with all in the fleet, No.15 was always immaculate. It is waiting to go 'Up The Vic' to Hanley. *(Author)*

Mr D. Rowley commenced service on Stoke to Newcastle in 1922 from Miles Green. Later Mr G. Rowley took over and the Limited Company came to PMT in 1954. His 'flagship' was this magnificent AEC Regal IV. XRE 235 was new in 1952 and had one of the last bodies to be built by Lawton. When new it was DP41F8 but later had three more seats added. It ran, mostly from Stoke Garage until 1965 when it was sold to Cowley. PMT only ran three of these superb chassis, this became S494, Davies had S496 and Baxter had C505.

PMT acquired ten of the new Weymann C41F8 Fanfare bodies on AEC Reliance chassis in June and July 1956. C5616/9, VEH 616/9, are posed at Hanley Park in Avenue Road, a favoured location in those halcyon days of no traffic on minor roads. C5616 was repainted in bus livery in 1967 becoming 'SN5616'. C5619 was refurbished and received a revised coach livery in 1965. Both were withdrawn in 1967 to Cowley. SN5616 went on to a contractor in Exeter. C5619 went on to serve Quayle of Liverpool for a year until it was converted to a stock car transporter in Cheshire. *(PMT)*

A unique coach in the PMT fleet was C5623, VEH 623 a Commer-Beadle TS3/ C41F8 new in July 1955. Beadle specialised in chassisless vehicles and the Commer two stroke engine was used in this early model. It was the only PMT vehicle to be taken home by its driver and was always known as 'Bill Bennett's coach'. Bill lived at Loggerheads and operated the Enderley Mills contract with the Blackfriars Special School in between. It was loaned to Yorkshire Traction in February 1956 and was withdrawn to Cowley in 1967. *(PMT)*

The interior of C5623 shows the transition from the traditional coaches of the thirties. The mirrors, clock and polished woodwork contrast with the 'easy- clean' plastics used as antimacassars. Tubular lighting has also replaced the friendly glow of the tungsten bulbs. The Commer preceded a modified batch of five in 1956 and they were very noisy but fast and economical. *(PMT)*

The crew of Austin's No 60 are no doubt sampling refreshments in Mrs. T's café on Pitcher Bank, Stafford having arrived from the wilds of Shropshire. WH 6854 was a Leyland TS7 Tiger new in 1935 which received, in 1948, this Harrington FC33F body. It was bought from Swarbrick of Cleveleys in April 1954 and lasted until 1962-a very good buy!

A 'dark satanic mill' forms the background to this all-Seddon IV/DP31RD of Smith's Tours of Waterhouses. RRF 291 was new in April 1949 and was withdrawn in May 1960. She was sold to Butter's of Childs Ercall and lived out the rest of her days in the comparative ease of the Shropshire countryside. *(Tim Machin collection)*

Berresford Motors No.19, BAU 811 was a 1935 AEC Regent new to Nottingham Corporation as their No.153. It had a NCME H28/26R body and was acquired in August 1951. Its distinctive wings were fashioned from sheet steel by Jim and Trevor Berresford. It was withdrawn in 1954 and was laid to rest in the Berresford depository for venerable buses which became a national institution amongst the bus fraternity. Behind, in this Longton Bus Station scene, is a Baxter TS7 Tiger on the 'Main Line' whilst a Stoke Motors saloon loads up for Heron Cross. *(Bill Jackson collection)*

Wakes Week usually meant visiting fairs and other showmen appearing to entertain the local populace. Typical of these was the Longton fair held on the old Alexandra Cinema car park. This fairly flat, un-metalled area has now vanished inside the Derby Way cutting. The author's new Ilford Sportsman caught this fine ex-United Bristol JO5G/ECOC B34R in 1956 soon after sale. BHN 254 has had its rear door sealed and the showman is sprucing it up ready for the visitors. A former Trent SOS was also with the same showman. *(Author)*

The conductor awaits the return of his mate in Tower Square, Tunstall, leaning on 'Reliance' Leyland PS2 Tiger/Lawton B35F. Reliance was a two vehicle concern owned by Mr .C.M.Dawson. The bus was used on the Tunstall to Newcastle joint service, with PMT, his coach was used on Race traffic. The Tiger, new in 1950 went to Baxter in 1958 and came to PMT in severely damaged condition in 1958. It received fleet number S503 but was not repaired and went to Lewis for scrap in 1959. Mr .Dawson was highly regarded by the BET Board and had a free pass for travel for many years after his little company came to PMT in 1960.

In 1956, Austin's, later trading as 'Happy Days', used to outstation a few coaches at the PMT Newcastle Garage. Here, 1939 Leyland TS8 Tiger BRG 184, new to Harding of Birkenhead, displays its 1948 Burlingham C35F body with a similar vehicle behind. No.57 was acquired in April 1954 and lasted until June 1962-another testament to Leyland products and a dedicated and skilled owner. After a series of false starts, the closure of this, the last PET garage in operation still, in 2009, hangs in the balance under First Potteries occupation. *(Author)*

When Hants and Sussex ceased trading, their well maintained buses were rapidly bought by other independents. Two were acquired by Stonier of Goldenhill, this being FCG 523, a very early Leyland PD1 Titan/NCB H30/26R new 1946. It left the bucolic scenery 'down south' and arrived in the Potteries in January 1955. It is seen in Dividy Road, near the site of the present First Potteries Garage at Adderley Green. The bus was withdrawn in April 1960. This livery had a green roof and lower window level with bright red bands. *(Tim Machin collection)*

One of the most important demonstrators to be evaluated by PMT was the prototype Leyland Atlantean with its rear engine and huge capacity of 78 passengers. 281 ATC was a chassisless bus, built by MCW, with massive internal partitions for strength. This 1956 view at Stoke Church shows General Manager, Mr. CW Wroth (in fedora hat), about to board. Also in the queue are Bob Bailey, Traffic Manager, Wilfred Inskip, Traffic Assistant and Norman Bennett, Claims Officer. Visible through the front upper window are the forms which invited comments from passengers and gave a chance of a reward. *(PMT)*

The first low bridge 'Jumper' to arrive at PMT in July 1956 although it was numerically the second was L6663. XVT 663 was a Daimler CVG5/NCME L31/28RD8. The class of fifteen gained its nickname due to the lack of confidence of some younger drivers to master the Wilson pre-select epicyclic gearbox. The 'Jumpers' were the first double deckers delivered in the short-lived red with cream roof livery. The Potteries atmosphere was not conducive to the longevity of the paint scheme. Later this bus, with some others, received Gardner 6LW engines. It went to Martin, Weaverham in December 1972, as the last of its class. *(PMT)*

The church wall in Bowstead Street, Stoke provides a rest area for L417, RRF 485, an all- Crossley DD42/5/L27/26R new to Mainwaring Brothers in March 1949. It was one of three Crossleys, the other two being the DD42/7 variant, delivered in 1949. The engines were troublesome and most operators, mainly municipals, changed them for the old but very reliable Leyland 8.6 litre units. PMT had lots of these in stock so the change was effected and they all ran from then to withdrawal to Cowley in 1960. The last of the trio was a highbridge, H419, allocated to Burslem, L417/8 were allocated to Stoke.

One of the routes worked by Rowbotham of Harriseahead jointly with PMT was the Tunstall to Mow Cop Bank via Newchapel and Whitehill. A typical Rowbotham Foden PVSC6/Lawton B37F, new in December 1947 was No.9, ORE 868. Fodens were among the first manufacturers to incorporate a concealed radiator, following the giant Midland Red. The fleet contained no less than seven Lawton bodies, including two rear engined Fodens, when acquired by PMT on 1st January 1959. No.9 was not operated by PMT and made its way to a showman based in Sheffield. The garage was operated as PMT Mow Cop for a short time and is currently the base of Paul's Coaches.

Thursday was Market Day in Sandbach and one of the PMT services was this unique express strangely worked by Fenton Garage whose L345, LEH 753 is waiting outside the Burslem Canteen. It was a 1948 Leyland PD2/1 Titan/NCME L27/26R. When new it was fleet number 373. It was withdrawn in 1964 to Frank Cowley of Salford. This batch of buses was among the best that ever served PMT.

H7700, 700AEH, was originally a Leyland OPD 2/2 Titan export chassis which the manufacturer converted to the new 30 feet length as the prototype of the PD3 Titan. It received this special MCW H41/33R8 body which was the only six-bay 'Orion' built. Its Midland Red 'tin front' bonnet made it the PD3/2 variant. It was exhibited in the 1956 Commercial Vehicle Show at Earls Court. The author looked in awe at this monster little thinking that he would drive it one day! The T&GWU were not impressed and it was downseated to H37/31R8. It spent its life at Burslem Garage apart from five days loan to Bury Corporation in March 1957 and was withdrawn in December 1970 going to Cowley in January 1971. *(PMT)*

The view from the front of the upper deck of H7700 emphasises its extra length. The décor was unique in that the maroon side colour was extended to include the window pans instead of the usual light grey-green. The latter had been a feature since the 1946 Brush saloons. The red leather trimmed seats had red moquette different to the 'Blackpool swirl' then standard. Just visible on the rear emergency window is the sign applied to the bus prior to the 1956 Show, which announces that the 'Metro-Cammell Weymann body is for the Potteries Motor Traction Co. Ltd.' It was the last new PMT open platform bus. *(PMT)*

PMT SN727, 727 AEH was an AEC MU3RV Reliance/Willowbrook B44F new in April 1957 and part of a batch of ten delivered in cream and red livery to be nicknamed the 'White Willowbrooks'. Seven of the ten, including SN727, were allocated to Biddulph for the Wells Motors subsidiary fleet to replace their elderly Dennis Lancets. Seen in Tunstall High Street, SN727 is returning from Over via Sandbach soon after 19th.August 1957 when it went to Biddulph. Wells was absorbed in March 1959. The livery changed to red on first repaint in 1960. 727 was withdrawn in 1973 to Martin of Weaverham (dealer) who resold it to an operator in Flint.

Loading at Smallthorne for Burslem and Newcastle is PMT H6658, XVT 658 a Daimler CVG5/MCCW H35/28RD8 new in October 1956. The bus has a 'Birmingham' front concealed radiator, which was an alternative to the classic fluted Daimler radiator. Once called the 'New Look' (N) front, this appellation fell into disuse once it became common in the early fifties. The photograph was taken on 5th.February 1957 and the bus was withdrawn in October 1970 to Cowley who sold it on to Barraclough, Carlton for scrap. *(PMT)*

Posed at Trentham is H705, 705 AEH a Leyland PD3/4 Titan/ MCW H37/31FD new in August 1957. After PMT rebuilt a 1946 Guy Arab, (H297), to front entrance and staircase, the MCCW organisation, offered the layout as an option on their 'Orion' body. The unusual side destination box was replaced on the first major overhaul. H705 was withdrawn in July 1972 to Martin who sold it to the Collettes and Cresta Dance Troupe, Failsworth. They sold it for scrap it in 1975. *(PMT)*

H704, 704 AEH, was a Leyland PD3 Titan/ MCW H37/31FD new in August 1957. It is seen at the Essoldo terminus for the Abbey Hulton services, opposite Hanley Town Hall in October 1957 with Driver Billy Evans at the helm. It was allocated to Milton Garage and soon became a victim of Abbey Hulton Bridge and lost its roof. After repair it served until December 1972 when it was sold to Martin (dealer) of Weaverham. It was then bought by Berresford Motors and returned to the area. It was withdrawn in August 1976 and was set aside in the 'graveyard' at Cheddleton where it lay for some time. *(PMT)*

On parade at Stoke City car park in October 1956 are the entire batch of PMT Commer-Beadle 'Rochester' C41F vehicles. C7716-20, VEH 716-20. The Rochesters were integral (chassisless) vehicles powered by the Commer TS3 two-stroke engine which gave a spirited, if noisy progress. They were set aside in 1968 and all went to Cowley. Only C7717/8 were used again, by K.W. Coaches of Daventry. Both were sold on again, finally being scrapped in 5/72 (C7717) and some time in 1970 (C7718). An identical coach is preserved by POPS member Roger Burdett. *(PMT)*

After its first repaint into the new, short-lived cream roof livery in 1956, H500 was used in a remarkable publicity stunt in 1958. It is seen here standing on six Wedgwood coffee cans! Posing self-consciously on the left are Driver Gerry Salt and Conductor Dennis Woodfint, third from left. On the platform are the Light Dock Foreman Frank Morris and Mr. Hall the Chief Engineer. Looking through the platform window is Bodyshop Superintendent Cyril Walton. Upstairs Lord Wedgwood and Claims Officer Norman Bennett are visible. This photograph appeared in national newspapers as well as magazines such as 'Tit Bits', 'Everybodies' and 'Reveille' of 28th August 1958. *(Wedgwood)*

Baxter No.16 was a very rare 'Unfrozen' Leyland TD7 Titan/ NCB UL27/28R. FTB 11 had been allocated by the MOWT to Leigh Corporation as their No.84 in December 1941. Baxter bought it in May 1952 and it ran, in Leigh blue livery, until it was sold to Viceroy of Saffron Waldon in May 1956. They ran it until February 1964 when it was set aside. In 1975 it was purchased by Colin Shears of the West of England Transport Museum. After some years in store, it passed to the North West Transport Museum. When they rebuilt their premises, it passed to the Manchester Transport Museum, in 2008, for restoration. *(Tim Machin collection)*

Mr. C.M. Dawson's 'Reliance' company operated from Newcastle to Tunstall and regular tours to race meetings. This classic all-Leyland PSU1/15 Royal Tiger, RVT 475, had its body altered to front entrance, (C41F8), by Lawton after a new coach was acquired for the tours. PMT took over in 1960, including the regular race driver. The author had his only drive of a Royal Tiger when, in 1965, he took it to Staniers for a Blackpool tour on the August Saturday holiday. Sadly, the Stanier driver had a mishap and SN857 was withdrawn. Its forward body was used to rebuild the Matador and the entrance was restored to the central position. The chassis was scrapped. *(Tim Machin collection)*

Seen at the garage at Alsagers Bank is Pooles Coachways No 8, TRE 843, a 1950 Maudslay Marathon III/Metalcraft C33F which was sold on to Sargent of Wrinehill in December 1963. In the centre is No.9, 938 CRE a Leyland PSUC1/2 Tiger Cub/ Burlingham C41F, on the right is No.7, RRF 474 a Foden/Lawton C35F. Pooles ran an intensive service to Knutton, also Newcastle to Silverdale, Scot Hay and Audley via Halmerend which still ran under the First Potteries banner in 2008.

One of the most famous coaches in North Staffordshire is seen at its base at Tean in the early sixties. New in November 1950, URE 281, an AEC Regal III/ Harrington. FC33F8 was never withdrawn from service. It passed directly into preservation when Lymers stopped trading, as Victoria Tours, and is in 'better than new' condition in 2009 with Ray Hine. Its distinctive 'fishtail' air conditioning fin is just visible. The author arranged for it to convey the 1972 League Cup winners from Barlaston Station to Stoke Town Hall for their Civic Reception on hire to PMT and driven by Mr. Aubrey Lymer. It had a 'sunshine' roof which was useful as the police had forbidden a double decker!

PMT once again found themselves being used by the BET as 'guinea pigs' when in August 1957 four of the new lightweight Albion MR11 Aberdonians arrived for Fenton Depot to play with. In November fifteen more arrived of which SN8736, 836 CVT was one. It has a Weymann Hermes B44F body, a later batch had similar bodies by Willowbrook. The Aberdonian was a lighter version of the already lightweight Leyland Tiger Cub and had an Albion five speed gearbox of awful capabilities. It also had poor brakes but despite this, SN8736 soldiered on until 1970 when an accident resulted in a one way trip to Barraclough, Carlton. *(PMT)*

One of five, C8764, 764 CVT was an AEC MU3RV Reliance/ Willowbrook Viking C41F new in March 1958. It was renumbered 764 in May 1971 and converted to OMO in June 1971 which entailed fitting jack-knife doors and red livery (DP39F). It became a trainer in March 1974 being sold to Martin, Middlewich in November 1974. He sold it to the Elim Pentecostal Church in Crewe who sold it in 1978. *(PMT)*

Stonier bought four ex- London Transport RTL class Titans in 1958. Former RTL 42, JXN 365 was a 1948 Leyland PD2(7RT)/Park Royal H30/26R. It ran until June 1966 and must have been value for money. The RTLs were deemed to be non-standard and LT disposed of them early much to the delight of many operators. They also brought a change of livery to the Stonier fleet, replacing the ivory, red and green which, whilst attractive, could not have been easy to maintain in the gloom of the typical Potteries atmosphere. In the left background lies the PMT Goldenhill Garage which closed in 1964. The lamp post marks the summit of the former PET tramway. *(Tim Machin collection)*

Poole's Coachways began in 1925 running from the village of Alsagers Bank up on the ridge above Halmerend, to Newcastle. The area had many collieries and the last in the North Staffordshire coalfield was Silverdale which lay on the main Poole's service. No.11, 672 KRF was a 1956 AEC Reliance/Burlingham B44F, several of which ran in the area with other independents. Poole's Coachways was a typical 'village' operator which had a loyal clientele. It was the last operator in the area to use Bell Punch tickets. *(Tim Machin collection)*

Greatrex of Stafford had a most interesting fleet with many unusual coaches. They also had a charming custom of naming their fleet after birds. Here 'Golden Eagle', No.69, TRF 927 a Foden PVF6/Heaver FC37C new in June 1950 rests alongside a Perkins engined Bedford OB/Duple C29F, MHW 936. New coaches in 1950 showed a flamboyance in style which contrasted with the timeless beauty of the classic Duple OB. The latter design ran in production from 1939 to 1952 minus the war years. 'Golden Eagle' was sold in April 1954 to Sugden of Birmingham.

The revolutionary Leyland Atlanteans were shown to the press in May 1959 prior to entering service in June. The first to arrive was L9773 which is seen bearing adverts at the head of another five on the church wall at Stoke. 773 EVT was a PDR1/1/ Weymann L39/34F and was to be allocated to Fenton Depot. These buses introduced the new livery with the red upper deck to the fleet. L9773 was withdrawn in December 1977 to Martin (dealer) of Middlewich who sold it to Carlton Metals who then sold it for scrap to Booth of Rotherham in January 1978.

The first of the revolutionary high-capacity buses entered service with PMT, in June 1959, from Fenton Depot on the 3 Meir-Talke Pits and the 6 Sandon Road-Chell routes. They were also the lowest double deckers at 13ft.3½ins. L9766, 766 EVT a Leyland PDR1/1 Atlantean/ Weymann L39/34F leaves Queensmead Road on a quiet lunchtime trip to Chell on its first day of service. On the left, Trevor Holmes goes home from Longton High School for lunch and shows an interest in this huge shiny monster. His interest probably stems from the fact that his father was Conductor George Holmes of Fenton Depot. On withdrawal from Stoke Garage, in May 1980, No.766 was bought by POPS who still rally it regularly in 2009. *(Author)*

POPS bought Atlantean 766 in June 1980 just after its twenty first birthday. It was in the livery suggested by the author, to commemorate the Centenary of NSTC, the direct forebear of PMT, in 1979. July 1980 saw the last PMT Atlantean in service run in on a Main Line journey from Meir Square. No.800, the last of the first batch was to be replaced in Burslem by a Bristol VR so the author took 766 up to Sandon Road where he had photographed it on its first day of service in 1959. It is seen outside what was then Sandon High School. 766 then moved to Meir Square to be photographed with 800. *(Terry Moors)*

Passing the Cheddleton premises of Berresford's Motors on a hot day is No.1, JX 6936 an AEC Regent/ Park Royal H30/26R. It was new to Halifax Corporation as No.201 and passed to Berresford from PMT, who had acquired a batch of these powerful buses in July 1954, but No.201 was surplus to requirements. It was withdrawn in May 1959 to A.M.C.C. (dealer) of London. *(Bill Jackson collection)*

Jim Berresford had an eye for a bargain and often bought batches of buses from the same operator. He acquired four Leyland PD1 Titans from Accrington Corporation in 1960. New in 1946, GTD 486 became No.35 in the fleet. Its body was built by Alexander to the standard Leyland H30/26R design. Jim ran them and some later PD2s in their original livery for a while. This was a deep blue with red and gold lining out (their Regimental Colours), which the town adopted as a memorial to the 'Accrington Pals' who almost all died in the fierce carnage in France in 1914.

The housing boom in the fifties led to a galaxy of old former buses and coaches appearing all over the country conveying builders to sites where new estates were to appear. North Staffordshire was no exception and to represent many local firms is this Ford Thames with unknown body working for Percy Bilton. TRF 412 is Staffordshire registered but has eluded the author as to its history at the time of writing. *(Eric Wain collection)*

Stonier No. 2, JXN 357 was a Leyland 7RT Titan/Park Royal H30/26R new in 1948 to London Transport as RTL 34. It was acquired in July 1958 and was withdrawn in September 1967 to Tiger (dealer) of Salsburgh. This commendable life was due to the early withdrawal of the RTL class by LTE. One of the area's 'characters' Conductor 'Dickie' James can be seen hanging on as the bus goes round the Albion roundabout in Hanley. Dickie was never to be seen without his black beret and his Scottish accent enlivened many a mealbreak in the canteen.

The iconic Bedford OB was not too common in the area. The only one in Fenton was CFV 167 a classic Duple C29F example belonging to Pyatt's Coaches who had a small garage in China Street. Its Blackpool registration suggests that it came from Abbots whose fleet always had a '7' at the end of the registration. Pyatt's livery was a smart grey and they ceased trading sometime in the early sixties. (*Eric Wain collection*)

Mr. P. Stoddard took over the business of Mr. C. Whieldon of Hollington in 1951 together with a licence for a Friday market day route to Cheadle. His first new vehicle was this Commer Q4 /Pearson C30F, VRF 607, in June 1951. It is seen in Uttoxeter by the Green Bus canteen and booking office. This unusual little coach was withdrawn in January 1960. Stoddard of Cheadle operate under the name of 'Swallow Coaches' (*Tim Machin collection*)

Berresford No.18, ORE 641 was a Leyland PS1/1 Tiger/Willowbrook DP35F new in December 1947. It is seen in Longton Bus Station on the Leek 'space'. For some reason, the City Council did not deem Leek passengers as being worthy of a shelter-even one of the notorious 'pneumonia pens'! The bus was withdrawn in September 1958 and was sold to MacKay of Tain. (*Tim Machin collection*)

Poole's Coachways held a licence for Tours and Excursions from Alsagers Bank (D.3451). No. 8, OVA 948 was an AEC Reliance/Burlingham C41F new in 1958 to Baxter of Airdrie. It came south to Alsagers Bank in April 1962. The classic 'Seagull' coach body had caused a sensation in 1951 when it was introduced on the then innovative underfloor engined chassis. The Reliance was a lightweight chassis saving over a ton compared with the AEC Regal IV which it succeeded. (*Tim Machin collection*)

Seen in Southport, Stonier No. 12 , YEH 913 a Bedford SBG/ Burlingham C36F 'Baby Seagull' new in July 1956, is flanked by a Bedford SB3 and a magnificent all-Leyland Royal Tiger C41C8, No.3, SPK 482. The latter came from Conway Hunt of Ottershaw in 1960 and was withdrawn in 1963 to Murphy (contractor) London N4. No.12 was sold in 1963 to Butters of Childs Ercall. *(Tim Machin collection)*

Stonier of Goldenhill bought No.9 in June 1960. It was a Bedford SB3/Duple C41F Super Vega. 932 MVT was sold, in November 1966 to Warren of Neath It is seen by the now demolished 'Ladies' toilets in the village adjacent to the yard. The SB3 was quite popular with Mr .Stonier, this was one of a pair bought new to which were added three more second-hand. He also still had two petrol SBGs and an OB in the early sixties. *(Tim Machin collection)*

Chapter 6

A man chases after Beckett JXC 212 an AEC Regent III/ Craven H30/26 new in June 1949 to London Transport as RT 1449. Let us hope that he doesn't want to go to Abbey Hulton as the RT is on a less frequent Ash Hall trip. It was sold off early, in July 1956, as it was a non-standard variant of the famous RT class. Beckett was acquired by PMT in March 1963 and its fleet of eight RTs were set aside. This one was sold to Cowley who passed it on to Heyfordian Services at Upper Heyford. They ran it until June 1967.

(Eric Wain collection)

Pioneer operator, Procter of Leek Road saw a bargain and bought a brace of these ex Birmingham Corporation Daimler CWA6/Park Royal H30/26Rs, new in 1945, in September 1950. Former No. 1419, FOP 419, is seen in Stafford Street, Hanley on the erstwhile 16 to Leek. The driver has placed a brick behind the front wheel and has walked down the dark alley leading to the notorious PMT canteen in Percy Street. 'FOP' was withdrawn in 1954, not an unusual lifespan for an un-rebuilt relaxed-utility bus.

(Tim Machin collection)

Smith's Tours of Waterhouses began operations in 1934 and held licences for the factory at Mayfield and to Leek on Market Day from Grindon and Waterhouses. VRF 169 was a Commer Avenger I/Churchill C37C new in May 1951. It was withdrawn in January 1964, a creditable lifespan in a far from ideal operating area. The cobblestones of Ford Street, Leek are astern as she waits to return her shoppers to the fringe of the Peak District National Park. *(Tim Machin collection)*

Whieldon's Green Bus Service went through a phase of purchasing examples of the almost indestructible Guy Arab II. This one is No. 42, GUF 163, a Gardner 6LW powered bus with NCME H28/26R body new in 1945 to Southdown as their No.463. It came to Uttoxeter in January 1957 and lasted until July 1962, a very creditable length of service, and a tribute to Guy Motors, Southdown and Green Bus engineers. The Northern Counties 'relaxed' utility body was metal framed and very durable. *(Robin Hannay)*

An unusual purchase for Procter of Hanley was this 1975 Bristol LH6L/ Plaxton C43F Elite, JRB 519N. It was new to Smith of Beeston and came via Millward of Hanley in 1979. It was withdrawn in November 1992. This Elite is fitted with a 'Bristol Dome' which became an option on non-Bristol coaches. Bristol RE and LH chassis had their radiators at the front so the best place for the destination box was on top. *(Tim Machin collection)*

Loading for the trunk 5, (later C84), to Chester is Crosville Lodekka ML925, 907 CFM a Bristol LD6B/ECW H33/27RD new in March 1958. The revolutionary Lodekka enabled low height to be combined with the upper central gangway replacing the uncomfortable low-bridge design. Bristol and ECW were only available to the nationalised Tilling Group. Crosville had a space in Newcastle Garage from its inception in 1932 and the new bus is in front of the Crosville Booking Agency in Newcastle. *(Thomas W.W. Knowles)*

The second batch of low bridge Atlanteans came in October 1960. They were slightly different in that the door windows now were above the side window line so the mirror could be viewed through the door glass instead of the windscreen of the first batch. The second bus in the batch is seen outside its home for all its life, Burslem Garage. L818, 818 KVT was a Leyland PDR1/1 Atlantean/Weymann L39/34F. It was withdrawn in 1973 to Martin of Middlewich (dealer). Graham Martin passed it on to Beaufort Air Sea Equipment, Bidstone as a staff bus. In June 1977 it went to Parsons of Birkenhead who scrapped it in April 1978. *(PMT)*

The famous Keele Street Pottery in Tunstall was associated and later absorbed by the Staffordshire Potteries at Meir. Transport was needed from the northern end of the city to the former airport hangers at Meir. Two buses were used, one for each company and presumably going by different routes. They lived in a muddy yard in Sandyford where the Keele Street bus is seen. Both were utility Guy Arab IIs/Roe UL27/28R from Plymouth Corporation. This one was former No.282, CDR 792 which was new in 1944 replacing a bus destroyed after a direct hit on the Depot.

(Bill Jackson collection)

Nickolls of Milford sold out to Greatrex of Stafford in June 1966. Their dark red livery is seen on HEF 510, a Bedford SB1/Plaxton DP44F new in 1959. It became No. 109 and was withdrawn in 1971. The acquisition brought stage carriage operations to Greatrex when the old established Hixon (Bank House) to Stafford (English Electric), D.1625, which operated on weekdays, was taken over. The main garage of Greatrex was in a cramped position in the Newport Road adjacent to the Midland Red Garage. The other was located in the Stone Road. *(Tim Machin)*

Berresford No. 5, JP 8153 was a 1950 Leyland CPO1 Comet/Harrington C31F acquired in June 1959 from Stopford of Manchester. It was withdrawn in June 1963 to Gleave (dealer) of Arclid. All was not as it appeared in this unique vehicle in the fleet. Trevor and his brother Jim Jnr. added a second gearbox! Once mastered, this remarkable vehicle could climb any hill and tow a broken down lorry if required. The late and much lamented Beswick chimney dominated the Longton skyline for years, now nothing remains of this iconic potbank. *(T.W.W.Knowles)*

The main express stands in Newcastle were on either side of School Street, near to the Hassall Street Bus Station. This 1960 photograph shows a real veteran in the form of Standerwick No.37, FV 6849, a Leyland TS7 Tiger built in 1937. It was rebodied with this Duple C33F in 1949. Many operators found it economic to replace worn out bodies after the war especially when the chassis were the ultra reliable TS7 and TS8 Tigers. The onset of underfloor engined coaches allowed the retirement of these grand old ladies and several survive in preservation. *(Thomas W.W. Knowles)*

School Street, Newcastle in summer was a hive of activity. Here southbound Bristol MW6G/ECW C41F, XUO 737, has two later models as duplicates to Cheltenham and the south, one of them in green Southern National livery. No. 2227 was new to Southern National in July 1958. It received Royal Blue livery and is seen in 1968 looking, as normal for this operator, immaculate. Several of these iconic nationalised coaches are preserved. *(Thomas W.W. Knowles)*

PMT Inspector Jack Bromley bids farewell to the driver of NWRCC No.168, CDB 168 of Buxton Garage as he sets out for home over the moors on a less than pleasant winter day in 1960. Its ECW B35R body is encrusted in salt and tells its own story of the hazards of this joint service, with PMT. Service No 49 formed part of the 15 Hanley to Leek via Endon timetable. The Bristol L5G would have been slow on the hills on a good day. It was new in 1947 just before the type would be restricted to the Tilling Group and was withdrawn later in 1960. *(Thomas W.W. Knowles)*

The joint Garage at Biddulph was opened on 9th August 1960. It was built by PMT on land owned by NWRCC. The Bristol K5G, AJA 177 was new in 1939 as one of a batch of 40 numbered 944-983. Its ECW body was replaced, in 1951 by this Willowbrook L27/26R and it was renumbered 457. The bus is seen in 1961 and is soon to be withdrawn. Peeping coyly out of the PMT half of the garage is the solitary Foden, H812, XRE 590 which came from Rowbotham of Harriseahead in 1959. The Booking Office was also joint and in summer, the express services were alternated between the two sister companies. *(Thomas W.W. Knowles)*

During the fifties several enterprising retailers decided to invest in an old bus, usually a small single decker, to convert into a mobile shop. The addition of a few shelves meant that customers could be visited at a regular time to save a trip into town. One in Stoke on Trent was this Bedford OWB which had been rebodied with this bus body after the War. JEH 330 was new in 1942 and would originally have had an austerity UB36F body probably by Duple. The council houses suggest the Meir area but this activity would occur in any of the estates of the city. *(Eric Wain collection)*

Whieldon's Green Bus fleet included No.6, URE 802, a Foden PVFE6/Windover FC39C new in September 1950. It ran until October 1964 when it was scrapped. This long life was despite Windover coach bodies having a poor reputation for longevity and may be seen as a tribute to the body builders at Uttoxeter and Rugeley. The coach is seen resting in the yard at Uttoxeter where the author always received a welcome in his youth when 'spotting'.

Working on the Associated Motorways service is Yelloways KDK 61, a Leyland PSU1/15 Royal Tiger/ Burlingham Seagull C41C8 new in 1953. It is seen in 1960 taking a break at the Four in Hand Newcastle. It was withdrawn the next year and was sold to Ashton of Wigan. The classic Seagull was named after the first customer of the new design, in 1951, Seagull Coaches of Blackpool. The Royal Tiger had vacuum brakes and the eight tons, unladen, of this combination needed a great sense of anticipation by the driver. *(Thomas W.W. Knowles)*

A hot but cloudy day in 1959 sees the usual myriad of visiting coaches to Trentham Gardens. Star of the show is Midland Red SOS 'ONC' No.2284, FHA 416 whose Duple FC30C displays its opening 'sunshine' roof and big wind down windows. New in 1939, this art deco masterpiece was withdrawn in 1960. They were often used as duplicates to the new CM5 coaches on the M1 express service to Victoria. A standard touring version, the C5, can just be seen with the ONC, which stood for 'ONward Coach'. They were the first diesel coaches in the fleet, using an 8-litre engine built by the company. *(Thomas W.W. Knowles)*

NWRCC AJA 120 was new in 1938, as No.920 with a B31R body. It was rebodied with this Burlingham B35R in 1950 and renumbered 366. The cold spring of 1960 causes her conductor to adopt the usual pose for a chat and a warm at the Rudyard Lake Hotel on the 9 to Leek. Apart from the trunk Buxton to Hanley route, 'The Western' ran over the ridge from Biddulph, where they later shared premises with PMT. The Bristol L5Gs were kept on, due to the narrow lanes round Horton, No.366 being withdrawn in 1963. *(Thomas W.W. Knowles)*

A good example of the co-operation at Biddulph is seen here in 1961 in Greengates Street, Tunstall. NWRCC EDB319 was a 1950 Bristol L5G/Weymann B35R and is 'ON HIRE' to PMT on the Biddulph via Park Lane Estate service. No.319 appears to have a standing load before departure, perhaps one was missing or it was Tunstall Market Day. The PMT driver would not have problems with the fearsome gearbox as he probably started his career with Wells (Dennis Lancets) or Rowbotham (Fodens). No 319 was withdrawn in 1963. *(Thomas W.W. Knowles)*

A busy scene in June 1962 in Albion Square, Hanley sees JXW 492, a 1947 Commer Commando converted to a loudspeaker vehicle circumnavigating the roundabout into Old Hall Street. It was a familiar vehicle in the late fifties in the area. Loading for Abbey Hulton is one of nine, ex-London Transport, Craven bodied AEC Regents, of the famous 'RT' class, bought by Beckett of Bucknall in 1956. All bar one survived to be taken over by PMT in March 1963 although they were not run. *(Eric Wain collection)*

The last front engined double decker to enter the PMT fleet was this solitary Leyland PD3/3/Willow-brook H39/34FD, originally ordered by Baxter as a low bridge bus in 1958, the takeover was in time to order a high bridge body to be fitted. H811, 811 JVT, was the only new double decker by this body manufacturer to enter the PMT fleet. It was destined to be based at Biddulph mainly for the 121 Tunstall to Mow Cop Bank except for the last few months of its life when it moved to Newcastle for use on the Hanley to Wereton corridor. It was withdrawn in December 1971 and went to Cowley in January 1972. He soon sold it to Barraclough of Carlton for scrap. The days of the big front engined bus were over. *(PMT)*

The Construction and Use Regulations were amended in 1961 to allow for an increase in length of buses to 36 feet from 30 feet. The width was increased by 2½ inches from eight feet. Conveniently this equates metrically to 2.5 metres. The first PMT vehicle to arrive, in March 1962, to the new dimensions was this Leyland PSU3/3RT Leopard/Plaxton Panorama C48F. C916, 916 UVT, posed at Trentham Gardens, was the first of a batch of five. Interestingly, the rear seat accommodated only four passengers instead of the usual five. It was converted to OMO in January 1971 and as No. 916 was withdrawn to Martin of Middlewich in December 1974 *(PMT)*

Pre-production Daimler CRG6LX Fleetline/NCME H40/33F, 899 UEH was new in May 1962. It had been used as a demonstrator before entering service with PMT. The Fleetline had a centre gangway upstairs but was of similar low height to the earlier Atlanteans. Many more were to enter the fleet even though Leyland developed a similar chassis layout later. The author was its last driver in 1978, when it was withdrawn, actually illegally as the tax expired at midnight and the turn didn't finish until 0015hrs.on the last from Tean! *(PMT)*

Posed at Trentham Gardens, when new in August 1962 is the first single decker bus in the PMT fleet to the new legal dimensions of 36feet length and 8feet 2½ inches width. SN921 was a Leyland PSU3/3 Leopard with Willowbrook B54F body. It was withdrawn in 1976 to Martin of Middlewich, the favoured dealer at the time who then passed it to a scrap dealer soon after. These first batch Leopards were slightly lower than later batches and so could replace Tiger Cubs under the notorious Heathcote Street Bridge in Kidsgrove. *(PMT)*

The huge length of a thirty six feet long saloon could be a daunting sight for a 'green' conductor like the author on his first conducting turn on the 21 Hanley to Gillow Heath. This route had to have single deckers due to the Biddulph Valley railway bridge at Whitfield and together with the 115 Tunstall route, needed the extra capacity. The early BET saloons to the new length had fifty four seats and SN 921, seen here, was the doyen of the class. The Leopards were very powerful but the steering was horrendously heavy and the clutch felt like one had a brick under one's foot. SN 921 lasted until 1976, fourteen years being a reasonable age. *(PMT)*

Burslem stalwart L286, KEH 269 has been seen before when she was seen at Clough Street Garage in 1954. Here, at the end of her life and despite looking well, she is in trouble. She has made it to Fenton Depot on a northbound Main Line trip and the crew have had a bus change and left. The Fenton running shift fitter has wound the blind a bit to show that it is not going to Talke Pits, 'PRIVATE' is right at the other end of the very long B1 blind. He looks anxiously towards Stoke from whence the Matador will soon arrive. L286 was withdrawn soon after, in 1963 to Cowley.

Having a break at the much missed Four in Hand, PMT's catering establishment in the former house, The Beeches' in whose garden the Newcastle Garage was built in 1932 is Standerwick No.25, new in August 1960. Part of the Ribble group of companies, Standerwick together with Scout, saw the new Leyland PDR1/1 Atlantean as a good way of moving people fast and in comfort down the new M1 to London. SFV 421 had a Weymann CH34/16Ft body so didn't have to stop at Newcastle, except to connect with other services. *(T.W.W. Knowles)*

When Leicester City FC lost the 1962 Cup Final, they paraded through the City on the last Midland Red SOS 'ONC' No.2286, FHA 418. Its Duple FC31C body had a sliding sun roof and the team could stand up through it. Afterwards it was sold for preservation to Thomas Knowles (Derby Corporation), Roger Dixon (Midland Red) and the author (PMT). As the only local owner, I parked her on the Dunrobin Car Park in Florence –no vandals then! I used to go to work in it on Saturdays, but lack of proper accommodation forced us to sell her to some Midland employees. Sadly they had the same problem and she was broken up. *(Author)*

Three line up at Trentham Gardens. Left to right are L971, 971 XVT, L975, 975 XVT and L961, 961 XVT. They were new in May 1963 and were Daimler CRG6LX Fleetlines with NCME H40/33F bodies. The 'H' signifies that they had, for the first time on a low height double decker in the PMT fleet, a centre gangway upstairs. They were withdrawn in July 1978 to Martin of Middlewich then Goodwin of Carlton for scrap in July 1978(L971), July 1975 to Crosville for spares (L975) and December 1974 to Martin then Carlton for scrap in February 1976 (L961) *(PMT)*

PMT L973, 973 XVT was new in May 1963. It was a Daimler CRG6LX Fleetline/NCME H40/33F and weighed, unladen, 8 tons 17cwts and 2qtrs. It is seen at Stoke sitting on six Wedgwood coffee cans with a delighted Lord Wedgwood in the cab. This was a quantum leap over the previous stunt with H500 at 6tons 4cwts.in 1957. The quality would be tested again with prototype Daimler Roadliner SN 1000 in 1964 and finally in 1976 with VR No.636.
(Wedgwood/PMT collection)

Austin No. 15, JUO 951 was a Leyland PD1A/ECW L27/26R new in 1947 to WNOC as their No.2924. It left the 'English Riviera.' in June 1962 and ran till January 1966, a goodly life due to the skills of the engineers of Plymouth and Woodseaves. The PD1A model was used as a supplement to the Bristol 'K' after the war by Tilling Group operators to alleviate shortages caused by the mass withdrawal of worn out buses all over the country. No.15 is leaving Pitcher Bank, Stafford for Newport in Shropshire.

Stanier Limited of Newchapel was a progressive family firm who became a PMT subsidiary in April 1965. The main service was Tunstall to Mow Cop Church with extensions up to Fir Close, by the famous folly of Mow Cop Castle, birthplace of the Primitive Methodist movement. No.1, RRF 64 was a 1949 all-Leyland PD2/1 Titan/ H30/26RD. The doors were added by Jack Stanier, a charming man and brilliant engineer, who later became Resident Engineer at PMT's Hanley Garage. He also rebuilt the body as evidenced by the window pans. (*Tim Machin collection*)

Having reversed off the road to the Castle at Mow Cop, Stanier No.2, TRF 61, all-Leyland PD2/1 Titan/H30/26R of 1950, contemplates its return down to Tunstall. Stanier ran as a PMT subsidiary until September 1965 under the guidance of the then PMT Trainee one Harry D Blundred (later O.B.E.). The author had many happy evenings on this bus and the others, after a days work at Stoke in the Traffic Department. When the garage at Newchapel closed, the work was transferred to Biddulph Garage and PD3s replaced Jack Stanier's immaculate fleet on the 120 service. After passing to Frank Cowley, No.2 went to Davies of Tredegar. (*Tim Machin collection*)

The 16 route passed the Cheddleton Paper Mill where Proctor Daimler CVD6/Massey H32/26RD, GBW 336, awaits custom. It was new in 1953 and was bought from Ronsway of Hemel Hempstead in August 1958. It was sold on to Ward of Adderley Green in December 1967. After a few years it was sold to a Basford scrap dealer who advertised it for sale in the Evening Sentinel. Sadly the preservation movement was hardly underway and this fine bus was scrapped. *(Tim Machin collection)*

The last PMT standard BET design on AEC chassis was also the first to be built by Marshall of Cambridge. SN979, 4979 VT was an AEC 2U3RA Reliance/Marshall B53F new in March 1964. The chassis was the same as the fabulous 'Commander' coaches but with a five speed gearbox. Allocated to Stoke Garage, this one often covered for breakdowns on the Ribble express service to London. This fine bus was withdrawn in April 1978 to Martin of Middlewich. *(PMT)*

PMT C989, 4989 VT was an AEC 2U3RA Reliance/ Duple Commander C49F new in February 1964. It was prepared at Central Works for the company's first entry into the British Coach Rally at Brighton in April 1964. It won all the major trophies as did the driver, Horace (No.1) Davies of Hanley Garage. Horace can be seen with the silverware at Stoke prior to a press conference. He was the top driver for VIP work for many years before his retirement .C989 was sold on to Concorde Coaches of Bugbrooke in August 1973 who withdrew it in March 1976. All contemporary drivers, including the author, agreed that the Commanders were the best ever PMT coaches. *(Author)*

The author drove this bus to Clayton for a House Magazine photograph in February 1965. L1026, AEH 126C was a Daimler CRG6LX/Alexander H41/31F. It was the first of the second batch of this type and was destined to be slightly infamous when it caught fire and was gutted in 1969. It was decided to rebody and Alexander had the capacity to oblige, fitting an identical body, to SMT specification, in July 1970. The interior had black seats and orange panelling like the contemporary PMT 'Standee' Fleetlines. It was fitted for OMO in August 1971 and was withdrawn, to Ensign (dealer) in December 1980. They passed it on for scrap in September 1981. *(PMT)*

Smith's Tours of Waterhouses acquired this rare Austin CXB/ Mann Egerton FC31F in December 1955 from Clayton of Stockport. DJA 298 is seen one winter with a sack muffler draped over its radiator grille. Many operators tried this in very cold weather using cardboard or even welding a sheet of steel to the grille. DJA was withdrawn in November 1961 and is believed to have been scrapped. (*Tim Machin collection*)

Blunder Bus! We did not know at the time, but the Daimler Roadliner was to become an unmitigated disaster and PMT had the largest fleet in the world! Here sparkling out of the box is S1048, KEH 448D a Daimler CRC6/ Plaxton B50F new February 1967 and withdrawn December 1974 to Martin of Middlewich and then to a scrapman at Carlton. The photograph was taken for the 1967 timetable cover at Clayton. The Roadliner should have worked, it had a low entrance, all seats faced forward but its American Cummins V-6 engine did not like stopping and starting all day. Its noise and smoke were legendary as was the bus's inability to stop! (*PMT*)

The author ran a series of features in the PMT House Magazine entitled 'Tight Corners' One notorious bottle neck occurred every hour during the day at Whitehill near the 'Oddfellow's Arms' a hostelry which no longer trades. The single decker on the 296 from Butt Lane to Mow cop Church, a former joint PMT/ Rowbotham/ Stanier service, crossed the 121 Tunstall to Mow Cop Bank. The latter was worked by a high bridge double decker from Biddulph Garage, usually the singular Leyland PD3/3, H811. Here the 1120hrs ex Tunstall on 28th. April 1966 driven by Driver F. Lawton, has just passed the Reliance en route to Mow Cop. Harry Blundred is chatting to the conductor. *(Author)*

Among Bill Hall's loyal customers was the Meir ACF Detachment who often used him for trips up to Blackshaw Moor Camp and other bases. Here, he is loading cadets opposite to the much missed Meir TA Centre, the author was also based there when O.C. 239(Longton)Squadron ATC. Bill is at the helm of 9920 UG, a 1961 AEC Reliance/Plaxton Embassy C41C new to Wallace Arnold. This unusual coach was 'set aside' in a lane near Rock End some time prior to 1976. *(Graham Potts collection)*

Wetley Rocks forms the background to Berresford No. 30, CRJ 358 a Daimler CVG6/MCCW H30/24R8 new in 1950 to Salford Corporation as No.358. It is working the erstwhile 16 to Hanley from Leek. The bus was acquired in July 1965 and it was withdrawn in January 1968 to Audenshaw Diesels for scrap. *(Bill Jackson)*

The author drove SN1120 to Trentham Gardens for its official portrait in November 1968. TVT 120G was a Leyland PSU4/4R/Marshall B43F. This Leopard variant was specially built for PMT for use in the hilly Cheadle and Leek areas and later became a generally available option. The batch introduced a smaller version of the PMT 'logo' which lasted until NBC days. When the fleet numbering system was altered in 1973, it became No.120 and it was withdrawn in 1980 to Kinross Plant (dealer) and then to Booth (dealer) of Aston. Sisters SN1127 and SN1128 are preserved. *(PMT)*

Mr. S. Duggins commenced operations in 1923 with a Lawton bodied Ford 'T' from Burslem. Later, Mr. T Duggins took over and he passed the firm on to his daughter Irene who became Mrs Belshaw on her marriage. The company later traded as Princess Bus Service from a garage in Clayton Road, Newcastle. They ran between Newcastle and Silverdale helping to force the closure of the PET branch tramway in 1926. The service was extended to the Park Site Estate and was shared with PMT. No.1, VRF822 was an all-Sentinel STC6/B44F new in September 1951. It was withdrawn in April 1967 to Scully (scrap dealer) of Newcastle. *(Graham Potts collection)*

The last PMT Service 177 Leek to Foxt journey is seen at Bottom House being worked by Hanley Garage with SN729, 729 AEH an AEC MU3RV Reliance/Willowbrook B44F. It was new in April 1957 in reversed livery and was loaned to Wells between May 1957 and March 1959. It returned to Hanley for the rest of its career which ended on withdrawal on June 1973 to Martin of Weaverham (dealer). The photograph was taken for the PMT House Magazine in May 1971. *(Author)*

A call to Stoke in the late sixties from the Leek Union Chairman to the author, who at that time was responsible for trying to cover as much mileage as possible on summer Saturdays, resulted in this photograph at Warslow (Greyhound). The Chairman was a leading member of the Leek Amateur Dramatic Society and was treading the boards the following Saturday. His turn was the highly desirable Leek Local 'A' which did the rural routes. The bus was OMO fitted SN 898, 898 REH the last PMT thirty feet long saloon, an AEC 2MU3RV Reliance/Alexander B45F new in April 1961. It was converted to OMO in August 1968 and was withdrawn in July 1976 to Martin of Middlewich who passed it on for scrap. *(Author)*

PMT started a new fleet number series in 1969 with coaches being from 10 to 100. Here No.12, VVT 912G, an AEC Reliance 8U2R/ Duple (Northern) C49F Commander IV, rests at Blackpool alongside an Alexander DP49F Reliance, SL1094. No 12 was withdrawn in 1973 to Everall (dealer).It served several owners until being scrapped in March 1982.A policy decision was taken by PMT to replace all coaches irrespective of age in 1973. The standard replacements were four Leyland Leopards and twenty Fords all with Duple Dominant bodies. *(Tim Machin collection)*

A good illustration of the difference in height of a low-height double decker and a high bridge bus is seen at the Dewsbury Road, Fenton garage of Procter. GBF 278/9N were Leyland AN68 Atlanteans with Alexander H78F with 'panorama' windows new in 1975. Alongside is Daimler CRG6LX Fleetline/Alexander H42/34F, AVT 249C new in 1965. The twins were the last double deckers bought new by the old established Hanley operator. *(Tim Machin collection)*

A change of management brought on a change in the buses of PMT in 1970. No.148 was one of a batch of Daimler CRG6LX-36 Fleetline chassis, which were to have been 83 seat double deckers. Perhaps fearful of the T&GWU reaction, they were delivered with this Alexander 'W' type B40D+29 body in May of that year. The 'standee' concept had been tried before, in 1953, without success and the Fleetlines were sold in 1977. No. 148 went to Citybus in Belfast and was one of many to be destroyed in the 'troubles'. Sister 147 is, however, preserved by POPS member Mark Plant at the time of writing (2009) *(PMT)*

A severe vehicle shortage caused PMT in June 1969, to hire in. Amazingly, Birmingham Corporation provided some magnificent Leyland PS2/1Tiger/Weymann B34F saloons. As usual for this great municipality, they were in immaculate condition which belied their age. They were new in October 1950! JOJ 252, No.2252 was actually hired over three periods: – 11 June 1969 to 11th.July 1969, 10th.August 1969 to March 1970 and 23rd March 1970 to 2nd June 1970. The author had the pleasure of driving Florence colliers home to Biddulph on several Friday nights and also returned 2252 to what had become the West Midlands Passenger Transport Executive, from 1st October 1969, in Birmingham as one of the last two. Several are preserved. *(PMT)*

One day in the late seventies, the Author took his young son to Uttoxeter. In an antique shop was a Kodak Brownie Box camera .This was purchased, a 120 film fitted and this is the result. Stevenson No.27, 219 BTP was a Leyland PDR1/1 Atlantean/ MCCW H43/33F new as No.219 to City of Portsmouth. It came to Spath in April 1976 and was withdrawn in December 1982 to Lister (dealer) of Bolton. It then went via Paul Sykes to J. Sykes of Carlton for scrap. *(The late Nicholas J. Cooke)*

Mr Bill Stanton set up his 'Better Class Travel' at Blythe Bridge in 1977. He soon moved to premises in Tean. Driver George Banks waits in ODM 100L, an exotic Ford/Caetano Moseley Continental C49F, outside the Gladstone Pottery Museum in Longton. It came from Davies of Dyserth in May 1979 and was later sold on to Douglas of Ramsgate. Bill and the author are currently (2009) workmates as part-timers with Wardle Transport of Burslem where his son, Keith is Manager. *(Keith Stanton collection)*

Seen sparkling in the winter sun of 1969 is the first of fifteen 'Jumpers' new in August 1956. L6662, XVT 662 was a Daimler CVG6/NCME L31/28RD8. Just visible is the reduced PMT 'logo' on the side, also the chromed Daimler fluted badge has been painted silver-grey. Mercifully, none of these classics received NBC 'Poppy red' livery. L6662 was withdrawn from Clough Street in 1971 along with all bar two of her sisters and went to Frank Cowley who passed her to a dealer in Gnosall. The River Trent is behind the wall and the Paint Shop is in the old Power House, still standing in 2009. *(Author)*

Latter day one man operator was Charlie Fowler based at Baddeley Green. One of his regular jobs was to be on hire to PMT on a Thursday contract for the Blind Social Club at Fenton. 509 DVT was always immaculate and was a Bedford SBG/Duple C41F. Sometimes called a 'butterfly' front, this classic design was familiar throughout the realm. This one had a claim to fame as it was the last petrol engined coach in the area. In 1977 the fledgling POPS hired it on a tour of Lancashire and Cheshire operators, the engine was almost inaudible. When Charlie retired to Australia to be with his family, his pride and joy was sold for preservation. *(Tim Machin collection)*

January 1974 saw the dawn of an epic era of the new NBC standard double decker in the PMT fleet. The Bristol VRT/SL2-6LX/ECW H43/31F introduced the new height of 4.09m and a width of 2.5 metres for double deckers to the fleet. Nos. 601 to 604 , OEH 601-4M are seen behind General Manager, Stan Morris and Chief Engineer, John D. Mundella. These buses were late in delivery from Lowestoft possibly because they had been built and painted in the former PMT red and cream livery. Red paint was found in two places under the poppy red when No. 604 was being refurbished at the Reliance Bus Works for POPS who bought it in 2007. No.604 went to Thomas of Porth in August 1990. *(PMT)*

The first of its type in the area was Bakers Coaches ARE 999M a Volvo B58/Plaxton Panorama Elite C53F new in 1972. This fine coach was brought to Stoke by Peter Baker at the request of the author, to show it to the PMT Chief Engineer, John D. Mundella. His comment was, "I wish we could afford some of these!" When the author moved to Bakers in 1980, the coach ran under the radio call sign 'Green 99' and was very much cherished. Later in life it received a new Panorama Supreme front after an accident and was re-registered 1513 RU. On withdrawal, it was again re-registered to CRE 745M.

The once extensive fleet of Greatrex of Stafford could be relied on to provide something of interest for the enthusiast. The sixties saw an influx of the newly available Ford marque. Typical is No.142, ARE 245J, a Ford R192/Willowbrook DP45F new in June 1971. *(Graham Potts collection)*

The joint Potteries to Newcastle on Tyne Express service on Friday nights produced a Northern General vehicle on Saturday, which PMT could use on one of their tours or expresses as it didn't go home till Sunday. NGT No.2531, ECN131E was a Leyland PSU3/4R Leopard/Marshall DP49F new in 1968. It is seen the next year on 'The Ranch' at Stoke with Stafford stalwart Atlantean L909. The latter has worked up on the 10 to Hanley for routine servicing. It and L910 were 'tweaked' to give a high cruising speed on the flagship service to Stafford. *(Thomas W.W. Knowles)*

At the time of writing (2009), this is the last time that PMT stood on Wedgwood. Bristol VRT/SL3/501/ECW H43/31F No.636, KRE 636P was new in February 1976. It weighed in at a hefty 9010kgs and so comfortably takes the record from L973 in 1963. Sadly, it appears that this exercise will never be repeated after four spectacular exhibitions of the skills of the Barlaston workforce and of the PMT engineers who had the delicate touch to enable six coffee cans to support a bus. No.636 was sold for scrap in May 1991. *(Josiah Wedgwood and Sons Ltd./PMT collection)*

PMT were regular contestants in the national 'Bus Driver of The Year' competition. The local heats in 1976 were held at the Newcastle Council yard in Knutton Lane. Here Bristol VRT/SL3/ ECW H43/31F, No 647, new in July tries the height judging test .At the helm is Driver Clive Pretty of Newcastle Garage while Terry Moors scrutinises. Clive had another regular task as Parade Marshall for the Mayor's Annual Remembrance Day Parade. 647 was withdrawn in April 1987 and sold to RAF Cosford as a mobile home after conversion at Stoke Body Shop. *(Author)*

Baxter's No.11, 203 BEH was their last new bus, in March 1957. It was a Leyland PD2/20 Titan/Willowbrook L27/28R which became L679 in 1958 with PMT. It ran at Clough Street and finally Stoke until December 1972.It was the last PMT open platform double decker and also the last low bridge bus in service. It was one of two trainers from 1972 and is seen in NBC light blue livery having been re-numbered T679 finally retiring at the end of 1976. It was stored pending a decision of the new preservation group, POPS, as to which trainer would be bought. As L466 was rarer, T679 went to Martin of Middlewich. *(Author/PMT)*

Berresford no.41, 1013 MW is a 1962 Leyland PDR1/1 Atlantean/ Weymann L39/34F.New to Silver Star, it was acquired by Bristol Omnibus for trials before passing to Super of Upminster from whence it came to Cheddleton with two others. The usual mount of legendary driver George Atkinson and his clippie, Betty Hazeldine, No 41 eventually was set aside and languished behind the garage until rescued for preservation. The author rode on it in 2007 at the King Alfred Running Day at Winchester. It is now preserved in Silver Star livery. *(Tim Machin collection)*

NBC dictated that only certain 'fashionable' companies would be allowed to have silver liveried buses for the 1977 Jubilee. PMT was not included and so decided to 'go it alone'. The result was this Bristol VR No.652, PEH 652R which looked better than the all-over silver buses. It was launched just prior to the Lord Mayor's Cavalcade in August 1977 at Stoke Town Hall. The Lord Mayor, Cllr. Ron Southern and his Lady Mayoress inspect 652 with L to R:- Robin Westbrook (Chief Engineer), Lord Mayor's Secretary, Driver Ray Hughes (Stoke Garage), Wilfred Inskip (Traffic Manager) and Dennis Weaver, (Divisional Traffic Superintendent, North). It was sold to City Fleet, Aintree in October 1990. *(PMT)*

In August 1978, PMT were allocated, by NBC, two prototype buses for comparative trials against a standard Bristol VR. They were given to Newcastle Garage where No. 700, (left) a Dennis Dominator/Alexander H43/31F, XBF 700S, and a Foden-NC/ NCME H43/31F WVT 900S (centre) are seen. VR No.686 (right) was renumbered 600 for the trials which were publicised as 'Operational Testing'. The VR was destined to be replaced by the Leyland Olympian as the standard NBC double decker. The Foden was stored for some years before being scrapped. *(PMT)*

The clean interior of the Foden-NC No.900 when new reflects the condition that it was in when it was scrapped, due to a short working life at Newcastle Garage. The 'NC' refers to the design collaboration between Foden and Northern Counties of Wigan. This disappeared after the American takeover of the pioneer Sandbach manufacturer. Of the seven built, one is a preserved runner and at the time of writing, one other is believed to survive. The Dominator was sold to Maidstone and District and VR No.600 reverted to its proper number. *(PMT)*

Above: PMT Foden-NC No. 900 ran spasmodically, but after the collapse of the bus building side of Foden, only seven Foden-NCs were built. WVT 900S was a Foden 6LXB/NCME H43/31F and never stood a chance. It was soon in trouble and as Foden had no interest, it was grounded for lack of spares. After being stored for years, it suddenly went to a scrap yard and a nearly new bus was lost. It is seen in happier times in Tunstall. *(Martyn Hearson)*

Right: As part of the 1978 celebrations for the 80th. Anniversary of the Potteries Electric Traction Company, it was decided that an Open Day would be held at Central Works at Stoke. Also a bus would be decorated, Bristol VR No.677 was chosen. The author was involved in the project from his first suggestion to the actual Open Day when he was involved with the POPS stand seen here in front of L466. *(Terry Moors)*

Bristol RESL/ECW B44F No.200, PVT200L was new in September 1972. Here it has been pressed into valuable service as part of 'Operation Green Cross'. This was two solid weeks of taking all the City of Stoke on Trent nursery schools out to instruct them about the safety aspects from a bus point of view. Here, the author shows Penkhull Nursery how to alight correctly. He did this satisfying task during his time as Private Hire Representative. The driver for that day was Ron Hadley, later to become Chief Driving Instructor at Adderley Green. 200 was withdrawn in 1981 and became a store at National Travel, Cheltenham. *(PMT)*

Climbing the steepest bit of road on the PMT map, Stonebank Road, Kidsgrove, in chilly conditions is one of the all-time classics. No.168 was the first of a batch of semi-coaches which were to be the 'swansong' of the marque. FEH 168J was an AEC 6U2R Reliance/Alexander DP49F new in May 1971. Six of these with the famous 'Y' Type coachwork were fitted with leaf springs rather than the coil type of earlier versions. This actually improved the ride of these superb vehicles. No.168 was withdrawn in December 1980 to Ensign of Grays (dealer) who sold it on to Calvery Coaches of Washington. *(Martyn Hearson)*

An NBC era publicity shot at the Sixth Form College car park, Fenton shows the latest equipment for PMT. Left to right: – No.102, XRF2X a 1982 Carbodies 7 seat FX4 taxi for the new Flexi operation, No.110, YRE 470Y a 1982 Mercedes L207D/Whittaker C12F, precursor of a huge rash of minibuses, No.21, GRF 221V a 1979 Leyland PSU3E/4R Leopard/Duple C46F and No.717, MFA 717V, a 1980 Bristol VRT/SL3/501/ECW H43/31F. No.21 later had tables fitted as the Port Vale F.C. team coach becoming C36F. *(Terry Moors)*

Seen at its launch, in July 1982, at the North Stafford Hotel, Stoke is PMT Flexi No. 101, the first of a pair of Carbodies FX4 HC 7-seat taxicabs. XRF1X is posing with the Misses Joyce and Frances Eardley (no relation) for the Annual Report of the National Bus Company. After experimental use as a bus in the villages to the west of Newcastle both taxis were used as private hire vehicles. In December 1983, No.101 was moved to City Radio Cabs, a PMT subsidiary. *(Terry Moors/PMT)*

The last Leyland coach chassis was the Tiger. PMT had the vehicles for both express work, with two leaf doors and coaching with a single large door. No.23, ERF 23Y was new in 1983. It was a Leyland TRCTL11 Tiger/Plaxton Paramount 3500 C48Ft. The Paramount came in two versions, the 3200 and 3500 which referred to their metric height. The PMT decided to call its coaching unit, 'ParaMounT Leisure' after this style of body, emphasising the 'PMT'. No.23 is seen in striped livery then in vogue for NBC express services. It was withdrawn to Kirkby (dealer), in October 1987, who sold it on to Arterial of Derby.

Berresford Motors usually bought buses in batches. Following on from a large bunch of Stockport Titans is this later example, one of several to come from Wigan Corporation. JJP 504 was a 1962 Leyland PD2/20/ Massey H37/27FD which ran with Berresford from 1977 to 1980. Wigan wanted its ratepayers to recognise their buses at night so, uniquely; they had blue lights on either side of the destination box. They can be seen in this shot taken at Wetley Rocks en route to Hanley on the famous 16 service. *(Bill Jackson)*

Chapter 7

PMT were the first BET company to experiment with minibuses when, in 1961, two Commer/ Martin Walter M11 vehicles were purchased. They were usually employed for private hire or as company vans until disposal in 1965. After de-regulation, PMT was bought by its management and a separate company, PMT Engineering, was formed based on the former Central works. Their early work was based on conversions of Ford Transits and Mercedes L608D vans. In 1984 the last of three prototype minibuses was built at Stoke. It was later to become fleet number MMM119, B119 RRE. It was launched in white and blue livery as a demonstrator and is seen with the large windows that the production vehicles would carry. *(PMT)*

Members of staff act as passengers in Mercedes L608D No.119. The B20F body was called the 'Hanbridge' after the Arnold Bennett name for Hanley in his world -renowned novels based in the Potteries in Edwardian times. Other body designs with Bennett names were the 'Bursley' for Freight Rover Sherpas and the 'Knype' on the Leyland Swift midibus. In October 1995, MMM119 was withdrawn and sold to Roberts of Cadishead (Dealer) for export. *(PMT)*

A truly historic bus is seen at its new home at PMT Cheadle before entering service in 1989. No.762, G762 XRE is an all-Leyland ONCL11/1RZ Olympian/DPH43/29F. It was one of ten in the batch, seven of which had coach seats. The first six of these were in silver for the 320 to Crewe and the last, 762, was the only one in the red and yellow 'zipped' livery, for the X38 to Derby. Their big Cummins engines were very powerful and the author never found enough straight road to find the top speed! It was renumbered DOC762 when the Crosville system of numbering afflicted the PMT fleet. Why is it historic? It was the last new double decker to enter the PMT fleet and is still, at the time of writing (April 2009) in service. *(Tim Machin)*

The immaculate fleet of Baker of Biddulph included a pair of Volvo B58/Plaxton Supreme C57F twelve metre long coaches. KRE 8/9V were later converted to various combinations of seats with tables and a toilet compartment for special private hire work. The author, during his time as Transport Co-ordinator at Bakers was surprised to find that, on their first inspection at Robin Hood Coaches test station, Plaxton had put the number plates on the wrong coach! This is actually 'Green Nine' KRE 9V, usually the mount of Driver Des Machin.

Double decker diversion on the Stoke to Bentilee route was under one of the 'Seven Arches'. This avoided the dreaded Glebe Street Bridge on this usually single deck route. Stonier's must have been short on this day as Berresford LAK 289G is running 'On Hire'. It was a Leyland PDR1/2 Atlantean/MCW H74F new to Bradford Corporation in 1968. It came from Metro, in Leeds, in July 1981 and was withdrawn in 1984. Stonier were part of the Berresford Motors Group. *(Martyn Hearson)*

Symbolism at Trentham as Stonier XTB 748N, a 1981 Leyland Leopard/Plaxton C53F new to Lancashire United, later Greater Manchester, rests before returning the colliers home. Dominating the scene is Hem Heath Colliery winding tower known as the 'Big A'. This huge structure surely should have been preserved as a memorial to all who worked in the North Staffordshire coalfield. Hem Heath had one of the deepest shafts in Europe and was latterly linked with Florence to form a 'super-pit'. The Leopard lasted long enough to be used by PMT although it did not receive a fleet number. *(Martyn Hearson)*

Waiting near the former RAF Hixon, now an industrial estate, is Stevenson No.25. MFR 41P was a Leyland PSU4C/2R/Alexander 'Y' type DP45F new to Lancaster in 1976. It was acquired in 1982 and later in the eighties, it was renumbered 65. It was sold to Edinburgh in 1993 but returned a year later to finally be withdrawn in 1998. The routes in the area had been abandoned by PMT who had acquired them from Mrs. S.J. Williams of Stowe-by-Chartley in 1936. The author spent many happy Saturdays in the sixties working from Stafford Garage on these routes. *(Eric Wain)*

The old established firm of Copeland are a familiar sight in the area with their immaculate blue coaches and buses. The tradition of naming the coaches continues to this day. Here, in 1984, 'Lady Margaret II' YBY 969G, a Ford R192/Plaxton Panorama Elite C45F basks in the sun. Her Ladyship was new in March 1969 to Moore of Southall and came to Copeland in February 1980 from Perry of Cardiff. She was sold in September 1984 to Madeley Anglers Club. *(Tim Machin)*

Seen outside the garage in High Street Goldenhill is one of the last two rear entrance double deckers in the area. 909 EUM was a Leyland PD3A/1 Titan/Roe H41/32RD new in 1963 to Kippax and District, one of the Wallace Arnold group. It came to Stonier from Hardwick of Scarborough in July 1972. On withdrawal, it and its sister were parked up at Berresford's yard at Cheddleton. They were mainly used on the Hanley to Bentilee services.
(Martyn Hearson)

Pausing in The Avenue, Kidsgrove is Stonier NPT 992M, a 1972 AEC Reliance/ Plaxton Derwent B55F. It was acquired from Bickers in 1985. The Derwent bus body was very well built being the last timber framed design built at Scarborough. The Stonier Company was a member of the Berresford Motor Group until the sad death of Jim Berresford when it came to PMT. *(Tim Machin)*

Passing Stonier's Garage in Goldenhill is Bill Hall driving ABO 145B an AEC Reliance/Harrington Grenadier C36F, new to Western Welsh in February 1964. Bill lived at Rock End near Biddulph Moor and operated as a coal merchant as well as a coach proprietor. His engineering prowess was legendary and is exemplified by the front six feet of ABO which actually came from CUW 560C a 1965 Grenadier, fitted after an accident. The coach is, at the time of writing, preserved by Mr. Phil Wilson. Bill's other Reliance /Cavalier is currently (2009) under restoration at the Reliance Bus Works after acting as Bill's memorial outside the family home. *(Martyn Hearson)*

A bit of rivalry in Bentilee sees a Stonier Leopard/ Plaxton Panorama Elite chasing a PMT minibus. No.MMM187, D187 BEH was a Mercedes 608D/PMT Hanbridge B20F new in 1986. The sad death of Mr. Jim Berresford brought to an end, in 1987, this episode and his Berresford Motors Group of companies came into the PMT fold soon afterwards. The minibus had been withdrawn by 1995. *(Tim Machin)*

Freshly painted in NBC 'poppy red' is OHU 766F an early Bristol RELL/ECW B53F new to Bristol Omnibus in 1968. It was one of a batch which entered the PMT fleet in green livery. These flat fronted RELLs were older than the indigenous later models, but were in excellent condition. No.206 lasted long enough to be painted in the privatised red and yellow 'zipped' livery especially for the POPS Rally at Clough Street. The author had an interesting fortnight when he was asked to survey all the PMT bus stops prior to a standardised new pattern flag being introduced. He used 206 then based at Burslem. Sadly this excellent bus went for scrap. *(Tim Machin)*

Stonier ran a Town Service in Kidsgrove in the late eighties and a 'Tuesday Only' trip is seen running through sylvan surroundings up to Acres Nook before returning via The Rifleman Inn and Stonebank Road. Driver Carl Jackson does this mealbreak trip in Seddon /Pennine B23F CFS 109L. This little midibus was new in 1972 to Lothian Transport and came to Stonier from the NCB in May 1985. It was withdrawn in 1987. Pennine Coachworks was owned by Seddon. *(Martyn Hearson)*

The much respected firm of Turner of Brown Edge, still known as 'Sammies' after its founder always ran clean vehicles. A second hand purchase in 1982 was ex-London Transport DMS 2028, OJD 128R a Daimler FE30AGR Fleetline/ Park Royal H 45/32F, new in 1975 as H44/24D. It is seen leaving Old Hall Street, Hanley for its home village. Turners were held in high esteem and after acquisition by First PMT, vehicles ran in Turner's livery with 'first' decals, a unique occurrence. *(Martyn Hearson)*

Mrs. Thomson of Hem Heath, Trentham was a charming, if formidable lady who was a strong member of the Potteries and District Omnibus Proprietors Association, of which PMT was a member. One of her later purchases was this luxurious ex- Glenton Tours of London AEC Reliance/ Plaxton Panorama Elite C34C, GYT 146N. It had been destroyed by arson before she sold out to Copeland Tours on1ˢᵗ June1985. Happily Copeland's have a policy of retaining acquired operators names on some of their fleet so 'Thomson's Tours' survives into the 21st.Century.

Here is a sad day at Kingcross House aka Longton Bus Station. It is the last day of Berresford Motors operations, marked by a board in the window of UTF 727M a 1972 Leyland PSU3/4R Leopard/Duple Dominant C49F. It was new to Ribble who passed it on to Crosville who sold it on to the NCB from whom Jim Berresford acquired it in May 1985. PMT continued to operate from Cheddleton for a while, moving in a few of their buses to fill gaps in the 'home fleet'. *(Tim Machin)*

Delivered in NBC poppy and white 'local coach' livery, No. 305, A305 JFA was a Leyland-National 2/ DP47F which entered PMT service in 1984. This batch of six was taken after a period in store at Leyland, presumably a cancelled order. The author did not like the 'Hydromatic' automatic transmission preferring the semi-automatic of the Mark I National. Here Driver 'Dougie' Hobson of Hanley Garage leaves Stone for the Potteries on the X60 limited stop service from Stafford. No.305 was withdrawn in March 1993 to Hatton of St. Helens.

Chapter 8

After the State-owned National Bus Company was privatised, PMT was subject to a management buy-out. The last new NBC liveried bus was Olympian 747, now preserved by POPS Secretary Paul Pearson. A competition was organised for a new livery and the striking red and yellow with 'zips' won. The test vehicle was Bristol VRT No.677, also preserved by a POPS member, before the definitive version appeared on Bristol VR No.653, PEH 653R new in December 1976 and Leyland-National No. 252, XEH 252M new in January 1974. They are seen on the Sixth Form College car park with red wheels. These were changed to NBC grey, presumably to use up stocks of paint. *(Terry Moors)*

Warrington of Ilam began running buses in the twenties. They ran to Leek and Ashbourne mainly on market day services. This charming Bedford SB5/Duple C41F was new in August 1981. Its index number, SFP 829X is unusual in that it would appear to have been registered by the supplier-in Rutland. It is returning home from Leek with its loyal and regular passengers after a visit to Leek Market. It gave excellent service to its owner being sold on to Stoddard of Cheadle in c.1998. *(Tim Machin)*

The trunk inter-city C84 was run by Crosville for many years until it had to be broken at Crewe, due to changing legislation on driver's hours, under Midland Red ownership. In the final days before the breaking up of the giant Crosville company, it used an attractive cream livery under the banner of 'Townlynx'. Old Hall Street, Hanley sees A154 UDM a Leyland Olympian ONLXB/1R/ ECW H45/32F new in 1984 leaving for Chester. Many of this batch were taken into the PMT fleet when the Wirral and Chester parts of Crosville were acquired. *(Martyn Hearson)*

Driver Keith Stanton carefully descends from Foxt down to Froghall in No.14, UVT14X, a Leyland TRCTL11/2R Tiger/Plaxton C53F of Stevenson. Keith was working a Leek to Cheadle via Ipstones which incorporated the erstwhile Foxt-Whiston Circular. This was one of the rural areas previously operated by PMT who either lost or shed routes to concentrate 'on core services'. A severe hump over a culvert precluded the use of PMT 36ft.long vehicles but clearly the Tiger had a better clearance than the Weymann Reliance driven by the author on the route check with PMT some years earlier. *(Eric Wain)*

August 1990 was very hot and Burslem Garage had been struggling on with Bristol VRs which constantly boiled up in the July heat. The new order for the 'Main Line' is seen here in Stafford Street, Hanley with a striking new bus. No.802, H802 GRE was a DAF SB220/ Optare Delta DP48F and is so new that it has yet to have its fleet number applied. PMT 'character', Driver Cyril 'Taffy' Evans has his usual welcoming chat to his passenger before departing for Meir Square. The radical Deltas were accompanied by Leyland Lynx buses which were a metre shorter but had a longer wheelbase. 802 went to PVS, Carlton in August 2008 for scrap.

Seen outside the Stafford branch of the Royal British Legion at Pitcher Bank is Midland Red Leyland Tiger/Alexander (N) B53F E29 UNE. No. 1749 was new in 1988 and came from Timeline in 1995. The Birmingham and Midland Motor Omnibus Co. had a presence in its most northerly Garage from the very early days. Its successors still do, often running on former PMT routes after years of joint operations and exchanging licences. Stafford is indeed, a fascinating bus location despite losing most of its long distance coaching operations after the arrival of the M6.

(Tim Machin collection)

PMT's Flexi operation required an open top double decker so No. 622 was converted. It was new in December 1974 as GBF 78N, a Bristol VRTSL2/6G /ECW H43/31F. It became O43/31F and for a time was re-registered 507 EXA. It later reverted to its original mark and was sold to First Devon and Cornwall in May 2005 in a deep blue livery. After use in the Penzance area and bearing its First fleet No.30001, it was acquired by POPS secretary Paul Pearson in March 2008 still bearing its 'Barbie' livery with attractive vinyls of the Cornish Riviera. *(David Farrar)*

Still on 'top link' duty in the privatised PMT 'zipped' livery of red and yellow is No.52 ,URF 52S a Leyland PSU3E/4R Leopard /Duple C49F new in September 1977. It is seen leaving Sheffield for Hanley and Newcastle on the X23 with Driver George Cooke at the helm. George, a founder member of POPS, was one of the top drivers for any special Private Hire work. A superb modeller, he used to visit schools with his tram and bus models to illustrate the talks given by the author. He is sorely missed by all who knew him. This highly scenic route was later reduced to Buxton from Hanley and is currently run, in 2009, by D&G as the 118.

Due to many low bridges in its area, PMT had many 'ultra low height' versions of the Bristol VRT with a height of 13 feet 5inches. The last of these was No.677, URF 677S, Bristol VRT/SL3/501/ ECW H43/31F new in February 1978. It is seen in 'zipped' livery under the control of Driver Arthur Gregory of Burslem Garage on the Thursday only 319 to Sandbach and Goostrey, the longest double decker route at the time. 677 later moved up to Pennine, then Rock Ferry. It was sold in September 1994 to Alpine of Llandudno who put in a Gardner 6LX. It is preserved by POPS member Dave Parry in NBC poppy red livery.

This lovely photograph depicts Knotty Bus No.1, OYU 573R a 1977 AEC 6U3ZR Reliance/ Duple Dominant C55F new to National Travel (London). It came to Knotty from Brewer of Caeran in 1988. In 1992 it went to Wealdon (dealer) in exchange for another AEC. Driver Tim Machin will have to be careful with this big coach on the lane from Longsdon to Rudyard on a schools run. *(Tim Machin)*